Facing up to Radical Changes

in

Universities and Colleges

EDITED BY
STEVE ARMSTRONG
GAIL THOMPSON
SALLY BROWN

**KOGAN
PAGE**

Published in association with the
Staff and Educational Development Association

The Staff and Educational Development Series
Series Editor: Sally Brown

Assessing Competence in Higher Education, edited by Anne Edwards and Peter Knight
Assessment for Learning in Higher Education, edited by Peter Knight
Enabling Student Learning: Systems and Strategies, edited by Gina Wisker and Sally Brown
Facing up to Radical Changes in Universities and Colleges, edited by Steve Armstrong, Gail Thompson and Sally Brown
The Management of Independent Learning, edited by Jo Tait and Peter Knight
Research, Teaching and Learning in Higher Education, edited by Brenda Smith and Sally Brown
Resource-Based Learning, edited by Sally Brown and Brenda Smith

SEDA is the Staff and Educational Development Association. It supports and encourages developments in teaching and learning in higher education through a variety of methods: publications, conferences, networking, journals, regional meetings and research – and through the SEDA Fellowship Scheme. Further details may be obtained from: The SEDA Administrator, Gala House, 3 Raglan Road, Edgbaston, Birmingham B5 7RA. Tel: 0121 440 5021; Fax: 0121 440 5022; e-mail: office@seda.demon.co.uk

First published in 1997

Kogan Page Limited
120 Pentonville Road
London N1 9JN

British Library Cataloguing in Publication Data

A CIP record for this book is available from the British Library.

ISBN 0 7494 2129 0

Typeset by Jo Brereton, Primary Focus
Printed and bound in Great Britain by Clays Ltd, St Ives plc

Contents

The Contributors

Sally Anderson is Flexible Learning Manager of the Educational Development Unit, Napier University.

Steve Armstrong is Senior Lecturer and Teaching Fellow with the Business School at the University of Sunderland. His research interests lie in the field of cognitive style, particularly its effects on interpersonal relationships in a work environment.

Philip Barker is Professor of Applied Computing at the University of Teesside. He undertakes research into human-computer interaction and the application of computer-based technologies to teaching and learning processes.

Sally Brown is an Educational Development Adviser in the Educational Development Service at the University of Northumbria at Newcastle. She publishes widely and runs workshops in Britain and abroad on issues of teaching, learning and particularly assessment.

Philip C Candy is Professor and Deputy Vice-Chancellor (Scholarship) at the University of Ballarat in Victoria, Australia. Previously he was Director of Academic Staff Development at the Queensland University of Technology for seven years. He has written extensively in the areas of self-directed and lifelong learning, and won the 1991 Cyril O Houle World Award for Literature in Adult Education.

Stephen Cox is a Principal Lecturer in Educational Development at the University of Coventry. In 1993, following several months treatment for stress, he was diagnosed as having cancer. After major surgery, he made a full recovery. In his chapter on stress he can therefore offer first-hand advice.

T Dary Erwin is Director of Assessment and Professor of Psychology at James Madison University in Harrisonburg, Virginia, US. He began research about college student development and learning in 1977, has authored numerous publications about higher education assessment, and assisted educators across many disciplines in the design of their assessment methods.

Paul Gentle is Head of the Department of Languages at the University of Central Lancashire. His current research interests centre on processes of culture change in higher education.

Wendy Hall is Professor of Computer Science at the University of Southampton, UK. She is Director of the Multimedia Research Group at Southampton, and also co-Director of the University's Interactive Learning Centre.

Ruth Heames is Head of the Occupational Therapy subject group at Coventry University. She is a state registered occupational therapist who prior to teaching practised in the clinical area of mental health.

Barry Jackson is Professor and Dean of Art, Design and Performing Arts at Middlesex University, and also carries Pro Vice Chancellor responsibility for encouraging autonomous learning throughout the institution. He has researched and written about student learning, particularly in art and design and his research interests now extend into the management of teaching and teachers.

Pauline Kneale is Senior Lecturer in the School of Geography, University of Leeds.

Mike Laycock is a member of Educational Development Services at the University of East London and is Coordinator of the University's Quality Improvement in Learning and Teaching (QILT) programme. He was formerly Director of the University's Enterprise in Higher Education programme.

Ray McAleese is Professor and Associate Director of Studies for the Department of Combined Studies, Heriot-Watt University. He was Director of the Institute for Computer Based Learning at Heriot-Watt from its foundation to 1993.

Bob Matthew is a lecturer in the Department of Civil and Environmental Engineering at the University of Bradford. Together with Pete Sayers he has spent many years devising and running problem-based group learning exercises and researching the issues that these exercises raise.

David Nicol is Senior Lecturer and Staff and Educational Development Consultant based in the Centre for Academic Practice at the University of Strathclyde in Glasgow. He has a particular interest in innovative teaching, learning, and assessment practice in higher education, and in collaborating with HE staff in support of educational projects in departments and faculties.

Alastair Pearce is Professor and Associate Dean (Academic) of Birmingham Conservatoire, the music faculty of the University of Central England.

Fred Percival is Professor and Director of the Educational Development Unit, Napier University.

Gerard Prendergast is the Flexible Learning Development Officer for the Gloucestershire Constabulary.

Pete Sayers is Staff Development Adviser at the University of Bradford. He works with Bob Matthews researching into problem-based group learning.

Lorraine Stefani is Senior Lecturer and Staff and Educational Development Consultant based in the Centre for Academic Practice at the University of Strathclyde in Glasgow. Like David Nichol, with whom she works closely, she has a particular interest in innovative teaching, learning and assessment practice in higher education, and in collaborating with HE staff in support of educational projects in departments and faculties.

Gail Thompson is a Senior Lecturer with the University of Sunderland Business School. She is currently carrying out research into various aspects of the student experience of HE, with particular emphasis on stress and its effects on learning.

Su White is the manager of the Interactive Learning Centre at the University of Southampton and is the university's contact on the UK Teaching and Learning Technology Support Network. She has taught computer science, has produced and developed multimedia training materials, and is currently working to establish an effective strategy to embed the use of technology for teaching and learning throughout the university.

Chapter 1

Changing Universities: From Evolution to Revolution

Gail Thompson

The last 15 years have seen a worldwide revolution in higher education. The university system has broadened to embrace a much bigger and more diverse student population, and the scope of educational delivery has been widened by the use of new technologies. A large proportion of the student population is less interested in enjoying the university experience for its own sake than in finding a job at the end of it. Many now opt for vocational courses, and following this trend, some universities recently have even started to offer degree courses in subjects which traditionally have been learned through apprenticeships.

Perhaps more significantly, there has also been a realization that completion of a course in higher education should no longer mark the end of the educational process. With today's world changing ever more rapidly, we all must constantly adapt to different situations and acquire new knowledge. Learning has become a lifelong process for everyone, and consequently, higher education is becoming more process oriented. It is also reaching out beyond the boundaries of the traditional student population into industry, commerce and the service sector; to people who perhaps would never have contemplated taking a formal course in higher education in the past; and across national boundaries.

The revolution has largely been the doing of government agencies. Around the world, legislation has been introduced to promote higher education while keeping costs acceptable, mainly for industrial and commercial reasons. The resulting changes have been far-reaching and quite startling in the speed at which they have taken effect. In the UK we have seen:

- the replacement of the dual system of universities and polytechnics by a single university system;
- a radical overhaul of the funding system, which is now based on performance indicators;

1

- a significant increase in student numbers (without proportional increase in resources);
- an increase in off-campus and work-based learning;
- changes in student funding, with a shift from grants to repayable loans, and more emphasis on family support;
- modularization or unitization of programmes of study;
- movement from an elite system to a mass system.

Throughout the world, similar changes are taking place; for example in Australia, where parallel processes have been moving even faster than in the UK, in the United States, and in South Africa and New Zealand, where similar trends have been observed.

These are changes that are familiar to all of us who work in higher education. The problems and issues raised by the changes, and how we can cope with them, have been the subject of much discussion, and this may sometimes have caused us to forget why these changes have occurred. Why, in particular, have governments taken so much (costly) interest in changing a system which has evolved over centuries and which has, until recently, served its students well? The cynics amongst us would doubt that it is simply from an altruistic ambition to build the perfect educational system, suspecting more political or financial motives. In fact, one of the main forces for change has been the drive for international competitiveness. Research shows that nations that have been most successful in terms of competitiveness over recent years are those that have developed a new type of educational system. Their new model is much more broadly based than the old one; it still fosters specialization in academic or vocational subjects, but now alongside this is placed competence in a range of core skills which generate adaptability, creativity, and the flexibility to respond to changing demands. The culture of lifelong learning forms the foundation for this new model. It is clear why this has happened.

- In today's environment, new knowledge is being acquired at a greater rate than ever before, so that knowledge gained only a short while ago is useless or obsolete.
- Advances in technology are accelerating at a rate unimagined ten years ago, and the workforce is having to change constantly to keep up to date.
- Jobs are less secure than they ever were. Gone are the days when a worker could stay in the same job throughout his or her working life. Now, most people will not even stay in the same type of job for very long.

It is easy to see that the traditional model of education, which in the main focused on the attainment of a discrete body of specialist knowledge, is no longer as relevant as it was. Employers now want their workforce to be flexible and innovative, expecting them to be capable of learning new things as the need arises. Knowledge for its own sake is no longer so important. Technology now provides us with a vast repository of up-to-date knowledge at the fingertips of everyone with the skills to access and use it.

Many universities, however, have been slow to acknowledge this trend. In 1992, Britain was ranked thirteenth on the world competitiveness scoreboard (Amin Rajan, 1993), and many researchers blame this decline on the educational system:

> 'a major barrier to upgrading and even to sustaining competitive advantage in industry (has been the way) the British educational system has badly lagged behind that of virtually all the nations we studied. Access to top quality education has been limited to a few, and a smaller percentage of students go on to higher education than in most other advanced nations.' (Porter, 1990)

In 1995, a report from the Paul Hamlyn Foundation National Commission on Education stated:

> 'According to the Organisation for Economic Co-operation and Development (OECD), the United Kingdom in 1992 had the lowest rate of participation of 17 year olds in full-time education in the European Community. The average participation rate for 22 countries covered world-wide was 75%; this country's proportion was 57%.'

It is little wonder, then, that the British government has acted with such conviction to press ahead with substantial changes to the system, and of course the picture will be the same in all countries trying to stay competitive.

However, I would not want to pretend that our educational revolution has only political or economic advantages. We should not ignore the fact that the very nature of our society has changed significantly over the last generation, and that this in itself has brought about a need for a review of the role of the educational system. Rogers and Freiberg explain it thus:

> 'Forty years ago the education of students was sustained by five pillars of support: families, culture, religion, community, and the school. The high rate of divorce, combined with the economic and personal needs for both parents to work outside the home, has shattered the ability of families to focus on and support the education of their children. Divorce, job changes, and housing mobility resulting from poverty have also destabilised the community. According to researchers, if current trends remain the same, by the year 2020 nearly 50% of all students will be educationally disadvantaged.' (Rogers and Freiberg, 1994)

This picture is starting to look rather gloomy for those of us in higher education. It seems that not only do we have the responsibility for the wealth of the nation on our shoulders, but we now also have to make up for the shortfalls in our society! We should, however, be cheered by the fact that the changes that we are seeing have sound educational principles behind them, even if they do sometimes seem to be secondary. We now have a system that is open to a much wider range of people than ever in the past, and at last there seems to be a widespread acceptance of the idea that the true role of educators is to show students *how to learn*. So much emphasis has traditionally been placed on teaching that learning has often been relegated to second place, and this fact has not gone unnoticed or without comment.

> 'It seems that, to most people, teaching involves keeping order in the classroom, pouring forth facts usually through lectures or textbooks, giving examinations and setting grades. This stereotype is badly in need of overhauling ...the primary task of the teacher is to permit the student to learn, to feed his or her own curiosity. Merely to absorb facts is of only slight value in the present, and usually of even less value in the future.
>
> 'Nearly every student finds that large portions of the curriculum are meaningless. Thus, education becomes a futile attempt to learn material that has no personal meaning. Such learning involves the mind only: It is learning that takes place 'from the neck up'. It does not involve feelings or personal meanings; it has no relevance for the whole person. In contrast, there is such a thing as significant, meaningful, experiential learning.' (Rogers and Freiberg, 1994)

With the spread of student-centred learning approaches, distance learning, group projects, and so on (admittedly introduced mainly because of the strain on conventional methods and resources) teachers are being forced into the role of facilitators of learning, and perhaps this is one of the major advantages of the changes we are seeing. This theme is addressed in several chapters of our book.

In addition, the higher education system is increasingly focusing on the importance of quality assessment, assurance and enhancement. The changes in higher education have resulted in educators being much more accountable to all their stakeholders, not least the students. Perhaps because students are now required to make much more of a personal financial commitment to their own education, they are outspoken in demanding good service. There has been a growth in formal quality systems which many would argue are cumbersome and hinder the educational process. Nevertheless, the systems have made education much more transparent, and as a result many positive changes have been made.

So, herein lie the roots of our revolution. It is a revolution because of the speed at which the changes are being made, and because it demands a culture change, to one of flexible, lifelong learning available to everyone.

Universities that fail to face up to the changes are unlikely to survive, and we are already seeing widespread strategic development of institutions to take them into the next century with the new culture and ethos. But change does not come easily. Higher education has a long history embedded in the traditional approach, the changes have no precedent, and they are happening at breakneck speed. Additionally, many of the staff within the system began their careers long before the start of the revolution, and are understandably still immersed in the old methods and traditions. Trying to change their whole approach while dealing with the heavier workload resulting from the vast increase in student numbers has been no easy task for even the most committed, enlightened, and enthusiastic academic manager.

It is therefore little wonder that there is a significant strategic gap in higher education. On the one hand, we have a rapidly changing environment demanding quite a different higher education experience to the traditional model, and on the other are the deliverers of education, finding it difficult, for varied reasons, to reject the established paradigms that have always worked in the past. Of course, students and staff alike are caught in the middle of this gap formed by the mismatch between demand and established practice, and many are finding it difficult to cope. It is this issue that we aim to address in this book. We look at the issues from four perspectives.

In Section I, we examine how technology is being used to support teaching and learning. While there has been a great deal written on this subject in recent years, the main emphasis has been on the learner perspective. In Chapter 2, Philip Barker takes a fresh approach by concentrating on how technology can be used to support teaching. His chapter addresses the important issue of how computer technology can be used to enhance and augment lectures, increase their accessibility, and improve their quality from both the staff and student perspectives.

Wendy Hall and Su White consider that the technology revolution has been very slow to take hold in higher education, largely because the sector has been so resistant to change. In Chapter 3, they describe how their own organization has overcome this resistance via their TLTP-funded Scholar Project, which has, they argue, successfully changed the culture of the university and allowed bold objectives to be set for the use of computer-based learning in their programmes.

Chapter 4 draws on experience from outside the higher education sector. Gerald Prendergast of Gloucestershire Constabulary presents an extended case study of how computer-mediated communication has been used on a distance learning course to enable a tutor in one location to facilitate the supervisory skills of distributed students. He shares with us his successes and his problems from his pilot cohort, and offers reflections on the role of the tutor in this type of learning situation. It is particularly interesting to look at the way that he describes how electronic communication media are able to support teaching and learning processes that we used to think were exclusive to the classroom. His case study shows us that support, good humour and friendly interaction can all take place, even though the students are dispersed and not always working in real time.

In Chapter 5, Ray McAleese asks the reader to think seriously about how we can make sure that technology is used to serve educational purposes, rather than education being adapted to suit the technology available. This cautionary note is a suitable way to close section one, for it is important that as we plan for change in our universities and colleges, we should be both pragmatic in the ways in which we use technology and visionary in the way that we embrace product change.

Section II comprises five chapters that consider the new strategies and policies that will have to be developed by academic managers in order to ensure that our universities and colleges can cope with the radical changes that we are facing. T Dary Erwin opens the section with a US perspective. This has the familiar story of budget cuts, increasing class sizes, and frozen vacant posts. He argues that the solution to improving this situation may be in our hands, explaining that a review of institutional assessment and evaluation processes is vital to provide the data with which we can support our arguments for additional resources.

In the next chapter Mike Laycock describes the 'QILT' process that has been adopted by the University of East London. He argues that this approach facilitates changes and improvement in his organization, in contrast to the traditional quality assurance approach adopted by most universities, which, he maintains, only serves to slow change and stifle improvement. The chapter describes how the whole institution is becoming involved in the improvement process, and the experience leads the author to argue strongly that university staff development should not be centralized but should be the responsibility of managers at a local level, who can ensure the development of all their staff.

Next, Alastair Pearce provides us with a really radical vision of the future. He suggests that modularization and unitization have not gone far enough towards providing a truly effective system of education. He suggests that that if we move to learning outcomes as the 'unit of delivery', students will be able to tailor their education to their needs and pick up elements that are most useful to them. He has also been brave enough to consider the problems that this might cause in university administration systems!

In Chapter 9, Sally Anderson and Fred Percival address the very topical subject of extending access. They describe two projects from Napier University in Edinburgh which are aimed at extending access to two groups of potential students: those in the FE sector, and those who do not have a traditionally accepted qualification, particularly among the unemployed. The paper describes how the two schemes were set up, and how some of the associated problems were overcome.

A chapter by Barry Jackson concludes the section on strategy and policy. He considers why academic managers have so far been largely ineffective in facilitating change in teaching practices within HE. His conclusion is that before organizations can change, the managers themselves must change to become academic leaders.

Section III includes a group of chapters about how academics can respond to the changing nature of students in our universities. In the first of these,

Steve Armstrong describes a practical solution to one of the problems of ever-increasing student numbers, with his surgery-based project supervision model. Within this chapter he also discusses his research into the effects of cognitive style on the success of student–supervisor relationship.

In Chapter 12, Pauline Kneale investigates the phenomenon of the 'strategic student'. Her preliminary research suggests that the expansion of the HE system has resulted in a growing number of students who are primarily non-academic in nature, and who are motivated by things other than academic achievement. Here she explores the causes and implications of this issue.

The next two chapters are concerned with the transition of university teachers from being knowledge providers to supporters of learning. Lorraine Stefani and David Nicol identify a deficiency in the learning culture of higher education arising from the fact that tutors and students do not share common conceptions of the learning environment. They suggest using a simple classroom evaluation technique to increase tutor–student dialogue in order to alleviate this problem. Further practical guidance is offered in the next chapter. Pete Sayers and Bob Matthew describe how they have adapted Blanchard's Model of Situational Leadership (originally designed as a model for supervision), to the learning situation. They explain how it can be used as a basis for reconsidering issues of power and control in the classroom, in order to create a flexible learning environment in which tutors adapt their style according to the needs of their students.

The final section of the book considers staff development approaches and methods that can help tutors face up to radical change in colleges and universities. First, Stephen Cox and Ruth Heames look at the effect that pressures in higher education are having on individuals' wellbeing. The authors offer practical advice on ways to reduce stress in students and staff, particularly by adopting different teaching techniques.

Chapter 16 provides a case study from the University of Central Lancashire's Department of Languages. This organization has embarked upon a structured programme of departmental change following the realization that the ad hoc changes taking place would not allow the department to meet its objectives. Paul Gentle describes how the programme, which is based on structured staff development, is moving the department towards being a learning organization.

The penultimate chapter of this section provides us with an overview of the issues of teaching and learning in universities from the staff development perspective, and suggests that we need to maintain a balance with academics who have a number of demands placed on them, as they are now required to be teachers, researchers, and managers. Phil Candy discusses how they might cope in this changing environment, and suggests some ways forward.

In the final chapter of the book, Sally Brown argues that facing up to radical change in universities and colleges is an issue that cannot be ducked.

We might as well therefore seize the opportunities provided, and work towards methods of curriculum delivery and assessment that are fit for purpose, reliable and sustainable.

This book gives an insight into how colleagues in higher education across the world are actively meeting the challenge of the changes that we currently face. We can not foresee future changes; the only thing we can be sure of is that we must continue to be responsive, self-reliant, dynamic and multiskilled. The challenge remains with us all.

REFERENCES

Porter, M (1990) *The Competitive Advantage of Nations*, Macmillan, New York.
Rajan, A (1993) *The Case for Targets. Skills for Britain's Future*, Crown Copyright, London.
Rogers, C and Freiberg, H J (1994) *Freedom To Learn*, Merrill, New York.

SECTION I
Using Technology to Support Teaching and Learning

Chapter 2

Assessing Attitudes to Electronic Lectures

Philip Barker

INTRODUCTION

Computer technology offers many new dimensions for the provision of support for teaching and learning. Until recently, most emphasis has been given to learners and the creation of more effective and more efficient individualized and group learning systems based on the use of computer-assisted learning (CAL), computer-based training (CBT) and computer-mediated communication (CMC) techniques. In the majority of cases, this objective has been realized through the development of supportive and/or collaborative learning mechanisms involving various types of interactive, technology-based environment (Barker, 1990; 1994; 1995). Nowadays, as organizational attitudes and infrastructures are changing, more attention is being given to the use of computers as support aids for teaching. This chapter therefore addresses the important issue of how computer-based methods can be used to develop, maintain and deliver electronic lectures as part of a more holistic approach to electronic course delivery.

Despite their many known pedagogic limitations, lectures undoubtedly offer a cost-effective way of delivering instructional material. It is therefore imperative that we think about the different ways in which computer technology could be used in order to:

(a) enhance and augment lectures;

(b) increase their accessibility (not only to local, campus-based students but also to distance learners); and

(c) improve their quality – from both staff and student perspectives.

With these objectives in mind, this chapter strongly advocates the use of electronic lectures as a viable mechanism for improving both the quality of lecture material and the ease with which it can be accessed by students. It is also proposed that this approach to lecturing can significantly improve the quality of students' exposure to lecture-based resources.

Essentially, an electronic lecture is one in which the use of a computer-based projection system is used to augment (or indeed replace) the use of OHP transparencies or a slide projector. Obviously, the use of lectures of this type allows a range of new types of instructional mechanism to be developed. Very often these can be based upon the use of multimedia resources that incorporate text, sound, pictures, animation and video material (Hofstetter, 1995). The various materials needed to create these lectures can be retrieved from a wide range of sources. Typical examples of these include: local resource packs (employing re-writable optical storage facilities or read-only media such as compact discs); and remote locations that involve the use of computer communication networks such as the Internet and the World Wide Web (WWW).

Because of the many different types of resource that can be used for their production, the design, creation and delivery of electronic lectures differs in many ways from the analogous activities involving non-interactive media such as OHPs and slides. For example, it is possible to integrate the use of special types of 'build sequences', transitions, sound effects, animations and simulations in order to illustrate particular points. Materials can also be pulled in dynamically from any source to which a lecturer can connect during his/her presentation. Naturally, using techniques such as these, lectures can become far more exciting and motivating than they have been in the past.

Bearing in mind the above, the objectives of this chapter are now to describe and discuss the issues involved in producing and delivering electronic lectures using currently available computer-based presentation packages. The chapter commences with a short description of our reasons for wishing to use this approach to teaching. Some different approaches that reflect current practice in this area will then be briefly described. Finally, the results of a student-oriented evaluation of electronic lectures will be presented and discussed.

MOTIVATION FOR ELECTRONIC LECTURES

Before discussing the different approaches to preparing and delivering electronic lectures, it is necessary to consider some of the important factors which underlie the growing commitment to this approach to teaching.

Undoubtedly, one of the most influential factors to consider is institutional policy and the hidden or direct messages that organizational fundholders pass across to lecturers and teaching staff. An example of such a message is reflected in an editorial which appeared in a recent edition of a journal devoted to learning technology.

> 'I was recently invited to give a lecture at the opening of a new high-technology lecture theatre at Leeds Metropolitan University. It is one of the best examples of its kind I have seen. Its impressive features include hi-fi surround sound, an enormous back-projected screen giving superb picture quality from either a VCR or directly from a computer for live demonstrations, online facilities, and the latest remote-control slide-projection equipment... Clearly, this set-up involved major expenditure. It was therefore presumably discussed at great length before the decision concerning such a long-term commitment was taken. But a commitment to what? To the use of technology in education, obviously, but also to the stand-up-and-deliver lecture. Typically, computer-assisted instruction involves a single student or small group of students sitting in front of a monitor, interacting with some software and self-pacing their learning. The traditional lecture represents the very opposite of this approach: large numbers of students taking notes, with interaction at best limited and at worst non-existent, and with the pace of proceedings depending almost entirely on the lecturer's judgement.' (Jacobs, 1994)

The message embedded in this editorial would appear to suggest a somewhat negative institutional attitude towards the use of individualized instruction and computer-based learning. On the other hand, as Jacobs himself suggests, it would seem to offer considerable support for the thesis that lectures (in one form or another) will continue to be used as a major vehicle for university teaching in the years ahead.

In addition to institutional policy, there are many other, more pragmatic reasons why staff in higher education might wish to use electronic lecturing techniques to support their teaching activities. Among the more important of these we must include the fact that, in general, electronic lectures are easy to produce, provided suitable authoring packages and appropriate automation tools are employed. Of course, we must also take into account the observation that, because they are in electronic form, lectures of this sort are easy to share with colleagues and with students; they can therefore be used to support distance learning and tele-teaching techniques. In addition, lectures in electronic form are easy to maintain and update; this important property enables high levels of re-usability to be achieved and, to some extent, allows us to combat obsolescence. Furthermore, provided suitable design and development strategies are adopted, electronic lectures can form the basis for the production of ancillary learning support materials (Barker *et al.*, 1995a; 1995b).

Because of their potential cost-effectiveness and their numerous pedagogic advantages, it is our belief that electronic lectures will become a primary mechanism for knowledge and information transfer within conventional establishments of higher education. In addition, as hinted above, it is our opinion that the electronic lectures which are used to deliver any particular course will also have to act as a foundation supporting the creation of additional learning aids for that course (such as CAL and CBT resources) which can be used on both an individual and/or a small group basis. Using this approach, the very same resources that are used to support local campus-based students could thus also be used by distant learners.

Of course, as a longer term goal, it is important to visualize the role of electronic lectures as a 'stepping stone' towards the ultimate realization of a totally electronic course delivery mechanism within the context of a 'virtual university' environment. Undoubtedly, by the next millennium many staff and students will teach and/or study by means of such an infrastructure.

THREE BASIC APPROACHES

This section outlines three different approaches to the preparation and delivery of electronic lectures. Each one differs with respect to the type of resource used and the kinds of facility which can be provided.

The Book Emulator

Benest and Hague (1993) describe the use of a powerful preparation and delivery tool known as the 'Book Emulator' which runs on a UNIX platform and incorporates a book metaphor. Therefore, during their construction and subsequent presentation (either in a lecture theatre or to an individual student at a workstation) the electronic slides used have much the same appearance as the pages of a conventional book. An interesting feature of this approach is that the slides contained within any given electronic 'lecture book' are accompanied by an audio narrative. Depending on how the slides are used – single stepping (within a live presentation under the control of a lecturer), browsing or continuous play (for private study by students) – the narrative can be either enabled or disabled.

According to Benest and Hague (1993):

> 'the primary motivation for on-line lectures is to produce a lecture that is of higher quality than chalk-and-talk. Quality gains arise from the production of electronic slides that are readable from the back of a lecture theatre, and that definitely indicate specific items without human hands covering up vital material in the vicinity.'

Bearing in mind these comments, as far as these researchers are concerned, a major advantage of electronic lectures is the wide range of 'revelation' techniques which can be employed (that is, the different ways in which the various parts of a slide can be covered and uncovered during an exposition).

They also propose that the ability to use animation within electronic slides is an important attribute which can make such slides much more meaningful than their static celluloid counterparts.

Although Benest and Hague do not necessarily advocate its widespread use, the continuous play presentation mode offered by the Book Emulator could be used to facilitate the automatic delivery of lectures – without any human intervention. Consequently, they have shown that this approach could be used to achieve significant productivity gains, for example, in lecturing time; the time saved could then be used to support a different study mode – such as tutorial discussion or problem solving.

Using commercial packages

A more conventional approach to the preparation and delivery of electronic lectures has been described by Anderson (1995). In his work, he outlines the use of a commercially available package for the delivery of course material. For a number of reasons he strongly advocates the use of Microsoft's PowerPoint (Grace, 1994). In addition to aiding lecture presentations, Anderson emphasizes how easy it is to use this package in order to prepare paper-based course documentation and student handouts. Within the University of Teesside we have been exploring the use of PowerPoint as an in-house standard for course delivery. Many members of staff now use this system as a means of delivering their lectures and making lecture material available to students (and other staff) by means of a local-area network. When asked to comment on his use of this development tool, the author of one electronic lecture course replied:

> 'PowerPoint allows me to produce handouts... copies of the slides... the students get these, 3 slides on an A4 page with room to make notes.... Production of the lectures was no slower than word processing slides, in fact I produced a template lecture and worked off that. The background, transitions etc I use are different for each but if kept the same then the process would be even quicker.... Student reaction has been positive... the colours, effects etc make the material attractive. I've seen students previewing the coming lecture and viewing ones missed.'

Many other academic organizations are also using PowerPoint in a similar way to that described above. Busbridge (1995), for example, is using this system as part of his 'Electronic Course Delivery' project at the University of Brighton; this involves converting 18 physics lectures into electronic form and then augmenting them with sound and video. Similarly, in his 'Lectures on Demand' project at the University of Ulster, Anderson is also exploring the problems of adding audio narrations to his PowerPoint presentations (Anderson, 1995). As is the case in our own work, audio augmentation is intended to compensate for the absence of a lecturer, for example, in situations where the electronic lectures are being used as a support for private self-study by students.

Using a programming environment

In the early work that we undertook into the creation of electronic lectures, we used a conventional object-oriented programming environment in order to develop our materials (Kowalewski, 1995). The authoring tool employed was the Asymetrix ToolBook system (Barker, 1993). Since ToolBook is a relatively 'open' programming environment, and because it supports OLE technology, the implementation of tools to support the development and use of electronic lectures is fairly straightforward. Once lecture material has been produced, it can be made available to students by means of a copyright free 'runtime' facility or as executable files (depending upon the version of ToolBook that is used).

When designing and developing our electronic lecturing support environment it was necessary to provide software resources that would enable seven basic processes to take place:

1. the creation and maintenance of a set of electronic lectures;
2. the storage of these lectures within an appropriate database facility;
3. the delivery of the lectures within a suitably equipped lecture theatre;
4. the augmentation of basic lectures using hypermedia techniques (in order to convert them into suitable self-study resources);
5. the provision of student access to the stored lectures;
6. the provision of appropriate student-oriented tools to support self-study using the augmented electronic lectures; and
7. the collection of appropriate monitoring data and usage statistics.

Bearing in mind the above objectives, a generic presentation shell was prepared using the ToolBook environment. Essentially, this shell consisted of four basic types of slide:

- *opening title slide* (giving the title of the lecture, its relationship to previous lectures and the name of the presenter);
- *overview slide* (which provided access to more information – such as the objectives of the lecture, its viewing statistics and an overview of the material to be presented);
- *conclusion slide* which was used to summarize the key points that had been made during a lecture; and
- *template slide* which could be replicated and used as a basis for creating each of the remaining slides that a lecturer needed to use.

The template slide consisted of a fixed background within which was embedded a number of basic reactive control buttons that could be used for navigation purposes. Two basic types of navigation were possible: within-lecture (from one slide to another) and between-lecture. Three buttons were used for within-lecture navigation. These were labelled: 'next slide', 'previous slide' and 'goto slide...'. The latter facility provided a mechanism for randomly accessing any of the slides within a given lecture sequence. The between-lecture navigation button was used to return control to a top-level menu facility that allowed users to move from one lecture to another. An additional background button labelled 'help' was available to provide basic information about using the system.

As a means of testing out and evaluating the package described above, we decided to convert a series of existing previously used OHP transparencies into electronic form. For this purpose the first ten lectures of a final year BSc course on human–computer interaction (HCI) were used for the experiment (Kowalewski, 1995). As far as was possible the first set of electronic slides created (Batch 1) directly mirrored the contents of the original OHP transparencies. As well as making direct copies, another sequence of 'augmented' lectures was also produced (Batch 2). The first batch of slides was intended for use by lecturers whereas the second batch was aimed at supporting students' self-study activities. Batch 2 lectures were derived from those in Batch 1 by modifying them in two basic ways. First, by converting certain words and phrases into reactive hotspots; and second, by adding 'information icons' that could be used to 'bring up' extra information relating to particular topics referred to in a particular slide.

STUDENT OPINION

In order to gauge students' opinions on our electronic lecture material (and this approach to teaching), two basic evaluative studies were undertaken. These studies were intended to assess students' attitudes and reactions to the use of the resources within two different contextual settings: lecture mode and self-study mode.

Study 1: Lecture presentation mode

This investigation involved asking the lecturer responsible for the HCI course to deliver some of his lectures using the electronic course materials. After the lectures the group of students involved were given a questionnaire to complete (N = 31; 52% return). This contained ten questions which were intended to solicit their opinions and views on: the quality of the presentations; the quality of the resources employed; and the potential of this approach to teaching.

Study 2: Private self-study mode

For this investigation the augmented electronic lectures were mounted on a server within a local area network. Students were then invited to access this material using PC-based computer terminals that were located at various points within the campus and remote from it. At the end of their evaluation of the material the students were asked to complete a questionnaire containing 38 questions (N = 63; 100% return). The questions were organized into five basic sections that dealt with: the quality of the online lectures; their ease of use; the quality of the augmentation material; the potential of the electronic lectures as a learning resource; and details of the respondent.

Main findings

When the questionnaires from the above studies were returned the data contained were transferred to a spreadsheet package and analysed. A detailed discussion of the results is presented elsewhere (Barker, 1996). Essentially, in both studies, students were very supportive of this approach to teaching – provided that copies of the materials would be made available to them. Of the lecture group (Study 1), 61% stated that they would prefer this approach to the use of overhead transparencies. A similar percentage thought that electronic lectures were a much more effective way of presenting course material. Interestingly, given the choice between having paper-based and electronic copies of the materials, the majority of the students (77%) showed a preference for paper-based copies compared to the 26% who would have preferred disk copies.

CONCLUSION

Despite their pedagogic shortcomings lectures offer a cost-effective way of teaching large groups of campus-based students. By using computer-based methods to support lecturing processes the quality of lectures can be improved. Furthermore, through the use of appropriately designed augmentation processes many of their limitations and shortcomings can be overcome. Undoubtedly, electronic lectures made accessible through the Internet and the WWW will form an important building block for the development of courses that are to be delivered through any future virtual university facility.

REFERENCES

Anderson, T J (1995) 'The Microsoft PowerPoint Approach to Electronic Lectures', paper presented at the Association for Learning Technology Annual Conference, ALT-C '95, The Open University, Milton Keynes, 11–13 September.

Barker, P G (1990) 'Designing Interactive Learning Systems', *Educational and Training Technology International*, **27**, 2, 125–45.

Barker, P G (1993) *Exploring Hypermedia,* Kogan Page, London.

Barker, P G (1994) 'Designing Interactive Learning', in *Design and Production of Multimedia and Simulation-based Learning Material,* T de Jong and L Sarti (eds), Kluwer Academic Publishers, Dordrecht, The Netherlands.

Barker, P G (1995) 'Interface Design for Learning', in *Computer-Based Learning in Science,* G M Chapman (ed.), Proceedings of the International Conference CBLIS '95, 30 June–4 July, Opava, Czech Republic, Open Education & Sciences, Opava, Czech Republic.

Barker, P G (1996) 'Making a Case for Electronic Lectures', Working Paper, Human–Computer Interaction Laboratory, University of Teesside, Cleveland, UK.

Barker, P G, Banerji, A K, Richards, S and Tan, C M (1995a) 'A Global Performance Support System for Students and Staff', *Innovations in Education and Training International,* **32**, 1, 35–44.

Barker, P G, Beacham, N, Hudson, S R G and Tan, C M (1995b) 'Document Handling in an Electronic OASIS', *The New Review of Document and Text Management,* **1**, 1–17.

Benest, I D and Hague, A C (1993) 'The Online Lecture Concept', in *Computer Assisted Learning in Science,* P M Nobar and W Kainz (eds), Proceedings of the International Conference on Computer-Based Learning in Science, 18–21 December 1993, Technical University of Vienna, Vienna, Austria.

Busbridge, S (1995) *Electronic Course Delivery,* Department of Mathematical Sciences, University of Brighton, Brighton.

Grace, R (1994) *Using PowerPoint 4 for Windows,* Que Corporation, Indianapolis.

Hofstetter, F T (1995) *Multimedia Literacy,* McGraw-Hill, New York.

Jacobs, G (1994) 'Educational Technology and the Traditional Lecture', *ALT-J: The Journal of the Association for Learning Technology,* **2**, 1, 2–3.

Kowalewski, S (1995) 'End-User Interfaces to Electronic Lectures', BSc Computer Science Dissertation, School of Computing and Mathematics, University of Teesside, Cleveland.

Chapter 3

Teaching and Learning Technology: Shifting the Culture

Wendy Hall and Su White

INTRODUCTION

There have been revolutions in educational technology before. Going back to the earliest days the evolution of speech and writing would be considered pretty revolutionary in terms of educational technique but as we live through the information revolution of the 20th century, comparisons are often drawn with the dramatic changes in society and education that were brought about by the invention of printing in the 15th century. Usually attributed to Guthenberg, this invention led to revolutionary developments in mass communication through the production of books and thus to the spread of knowledge throughout the civilized world. It had the effect of dramatically enlarging the number of literate people, so that civilized society today considers itself to be failing if any significant proportion of its population is illiterate.

Any revolutionary development has its counterpart in a resistance movement. The Luddites of the industrial revolution have become part of everyday language in representing the futility of opposition in the face of inevitable progression. It may seem ludicrous to us now but in the early days of the printed book there were many who were against this development. This quote about the Duke of Urbino's library in the 15th century is taken from Steinberg's *Five Hundred Years of Printing*:

> 'all books (in his library) were superlatively written with the pen, had there been one printed book, it would have been ashamed in such company' (Steinberg, 1955).

It was also a long while before businesses developed that made any sort of profit out of printing. What was the development that was the catalyst for the creation of the mass market for printed books? Some might argue it was an idea of Aldus of Venice at the end of the 15th century to produce a series of books that were 'scholarly, compact and cheap'. He had the idea to print editions of books 1,000 copies at a time rather than the more normal 100 copies. This was in order to make it economically viable, using smaller and less intricate print types and producing much smaller and more compact books. He essentially produced the first 'pocket' or 'student' editions and made books truly portable. They were also cheaper and thus more accessible to the general population. Before this development, teachers may well have been reluctant to use printed books with their students.

In this chapter we wish to explore why, despite endless talk about their considerable potential, the new information technologies are not yet part of the everyday culture of teaching and learning in higher education, and what are the factors that might change this situation.

COMPUTER-ASSISTED LEARNING: BREAKING DOWN THE BARRIERS

We must ask ourselves why, after so many years of hype and promise, the use of IT in education is still not a mainstream activity. The inertia in the system seems to be just too great; we all know how long it takes to bring about any significant changes in educational methodology, but there is also personal inertia among members of staff. The barriers to the effective use of computer-assisted learning in the classroom or lecture hall seem sometimes to grow bigger as time passes, even though the cost of the technology continues to decrease dramatically and the ease of use of both the hardware and software has improved significantly in the last decade.

It is easy to cite a list of barriers that prevent staff from actively embracing the new technologies in their teaching. In terms of content, there is a very strong 'not-invented here' syndrome; we all want to put our own spin on the way we teach and the tutorial content we provide for our students. Today's educational software is often very much a take-it-or-leave-it package: difficult to customize or modify or link to other material, whether our own lecture notes or third party applications. It seems to become quickly outdated and is often only available for systems that are incompatible with the ones we have to use. Because of this, many staff or teaching groups feel the need to constantly re-invent the wheel and think they have to learn how to use authoring packages and embark on their own multimedia production activities in order to use the technology effectively in their teaching. This is very time consuming and expensive in terms of resources and many groups give up at this point deciding that they just don't have the time or the energy to devote to such activities, and anyway what justification is there that it would make their teaching more effective? Following these sorts of arguments, many people never start. This means they aren't providing a driving factor on institutions to provide the resources required to support such activities (the hardware and network infrastructure), which means that staff are further discouraged from actively seeking to incorporate new technology into their teaching, and so the vicious circle goes on. Meanwhile, the poor students who have no such inhibitions about using new technology in any aspect of their work are left struggling against inadequate resource provision.

To break out of this circle, we believe the major change required is a change in perception, in which we recognize that the application of new technology in teaching and learning is not so very different from what we do already. The preparation of traditional lectures and teaching materials is essentially a resource-based activity. Teachers collect resources which they re-use as appropriate in conjunction with their own material. Applying this approach to the development of computer-based teaching material is a natural progression from current practices and can help break down some of the perceived barriers that prevent staff from utilizing computers in support of their teaching. Resources can include standard multimedia documents but also interactive components such as interactive discussion on the Internet, guided tutorials and simulations. As more such resources become available, staff will be encouraged to make everyday use of them. Authoring environments will enable integration of new instructional components into customized and personalized systems.

Reusability is key to the effective use of multimedia. Interactive multimedia resources are expensive and time consuming to produce on many different levels. We need to get over the barriers of the 'not invented here' syndrome and the continual reinvention of multimedia wheels. Multimedia producers, teams of academics, technology experts, graphics designers and publishers, should make material available on CD-ROM or over the network, and multimedia consumers, both teachers and students, should be able to incorporate those resources into their own teaching and learning environments. Multimedia systems must be shown to be educationally effective. At the very least they must give the students the same quality of experience as they have with traditional teaching methods. At best they will enhance and improve the students' quality of learning. When it works well, staff will have more time to devote to both research and to working with students on a one to one basis.

Technological barriers, such as inter-operability across different hardware platforms and lack of resources for student use, are important issues, but they are likely to be overcome at a much faster pace than the cultural issues. Large-scale changes in educational practice require very long timescales. Traditional authoring tools do not encourage the *modus operandi* described above. On the contrary, they more naturally promote the development of stand-alone applications that are isolated from standard desktop applications, and are extremely difficult to modify, customize, update or extend because the structure of the application is mostly embedded in the data to which it refers. We have to create software development environments that enable easy customization and extension of published resources and the integration of the resulting teaching and learning materials into the everyday computer-based working environment.

We use the open hypermedia system Microcosm, which was developed at Southampton, to facilitate the development of multimedia learning environments using this resource-based approach (Davis *et al.*, 1992, Hall *et al.*, 1996). It encourages the creation of common sets of resource material with different sets of links (and therefore different paths through the material) for different users as well as re-usability of material and customization by both staff and students. Above all it permits integration with standard desktop applications and a wide variety of resource material such as online reference material, CD-ROMs, information accessible on the Internet, etc.

We encourage staff who are hesitant about committing whole-heartedly to using multimedia in their teaching to begin by building their own resource base of material for their students to access. This can include their own lecture notes, any relevant online material that they can identify, other material that they have copyright permission to make available to students electronically and courseware produced by other academics such as by the consortia groups funded by the HEFC's Teaching and Learning Technology Programme (TLTP). When a member of staff has become more confident, they can be encouraged if they want to create multimedia courseware, such as question-and-answer material, simulations and guided tutorials, all of which can refer to and draw on material in the resource base. We don't expect the majority of teaching staff to want to become multimedia courseware producers, however. The more enthusiastic will want to do this but the majority will be happy to either specify what they want to a specialist team (providing the resources to do this are available) or to buy in suitable material produced by specialist teams such as TLTP consortia just as we buy in textbooks today. The resource-based approach enables staff to readily integrate such courseware into a customized learning environment and sets of resources that they have provided for their students. Examples of this type of material that have been developed at Southampton are described in Woolf and Hall (1995) and Hall *et al.* (1995).

REASONS TO GET STARTED

Until there is a critical mass of suitable material and evidence of its effective use by staff and students, there are still going to be many staff who are not encouraged to incorporate new technology into their teaching even using the easy step-by-step approach of resource-based learning. The conflicting pressures on their time are just too great to make it seem worth their while.

There are some very pragmatic reasons why no member of staff can or should ignore the impact of new technology in education. Firstly, we live in a world in which developments in technology are affecting everything about the way we live and work. Words like 'teleworking', 'telematics', 'interactive television', 'video on demand' and the 'information superhighway' are now part of everyday vocabulary. There is also an inevitable drift that no one can ignore. Wordprocessors, graphics packages and databases, for example, are used as standard tools by many in education. Increasingly students will expect us to use e-mail and the Internet as readily as they do, and in the future, techniques such as video conferencing will become much more commonplace. We are already witnessing a complete revolution in the way we publish and access research information as more and more journals are available electronically, and almost anyone with an e-mail address has become their own electronic publisher by creating a home page on the Web.

There are practical reasons as well. Increasing student numbers and the range of ability and background of students on our courses are forcing us to redesign the curriculum and teaching methods. The use of technology can and does provide solutions to some of these problems. Finally, there are political pressures such as teaching quality and research audits, which again are forcing us to consider the ways in which technology can improve the quality and effectiveness of what we do for a lower per capita cost.

No member of staff can put their head in the sand and ignore the use of technology in education. However, in the long run it is examples of best practice that might have the greatest impact. Such radical changes in educational methodology cannot be brought about by individuals and small groups working in isolation. The TLTP initiative has shown ways in which institutional barriers can be broken down, but institutions themselves must take an holistic approach to managing the change. Here we discuss the work that has been undertaken at Southampton in this respect.

THE SCHOLAR PROJECT AT THE UNIVERSITY OF SOUTHAMPTON

The Scholar Project at the University of Southampton was a new initiative establishing a service unit called the Interactive Learning Centre (ILC) to support and advise staff in the production and integration of computer-based learning materials into the established academic programme. It built on a number of strengths: extending existing expertise in teaching and learning technology (Sprunt, 1989); enhancing collaborations between key service areas; and establishing a desire to develop innovative resource based learning materials using the hypermedia system, Microcosm, in a way that is especially relevant to the educational needs of higher education. There was no real centre for the development of computer-facilitated learning in the university prior to the Teaching and Learning Technology Programme (TLTP). However, the project extended existing small-scale staff development and support and production activities within the Teaching Support and Media Services Department which arose from the Interactive Video in Higher Education initiative funded by the university.

The University of Southampton has always been strong in the application of technology to education, as demonstrated by the highly successful track record of the Teaching Support and Media Services (formally Teaching Media) and the associated Video Production Unit. An embryonic Interactive Learning Centre was established at the university in 1989 as a result of the recommendations made by the report (Mathias, 1992) on Interactive Video in Higher Education at the end of this two-year project at the university. It also built upon many different initiatives to develop computer-based teaching and learning materials which had arisen around the campus out of interest, and both internal and external funding. It was established in close collaboration with the University Library, Computing Services and the Department of Electronics and Computer Science.

There was strong evidence of high-level institutional support and commitment, backed up by strategic involvement in and commitment to the project from all three key service areas, which collaborate under the single umbrella of the University of Southampton Information Group (USING). Our successful bid for funding from TLTP for an institutional project enabled us to build on these early foundations and to firmly establish the ILC at Southampton as the focal point of teaching and learning activity at the university. From the beginning this work has had three important components: provision of courses for staff development and awareness; funding and support for pump-priming projects; and development of the necessary infrastructure to support teaching and learning activities across the campus. These three areas reflected university inputs to the project, and were broad areas to be targeted for change to provide leverage in the task of shifting the culture towards the use of multimedia and hypermedia as an integral part of academic life.

Key initial tasks were to define two policy documents, one for the Scholar Project itself, and one for the Interactive Learning Centre. These documents served to clarify the aims and objectives of the project and establish a framework for the advice, consultancy and support services which were to be provided by the Interactive Learning Centre. They also served to establish an understanding of the project targets among university management. Like all TLTP projects, the Scholar Project was tasked with the objective of creating project deliverables rather than engaging in research. However, the project benefited from working in a wider context of a time for change focusing on issues of implementation in institutions. This is evidenced by publications such as the McFarlane Report (1992), and Diana Laurillard's *Rethinking University Education* (1993).

The increased profile of teaching and learning innovations achieved through project activities, combined with the wider research focus and departmental objectives related to teaching quality assessment, may have helped establish a credible context for practical teaching and learning initiatives within a traditional university such as Southampton. The university places strong emphasis on its research activities and the challenges of providing the technical infrastructure to deliver technology-based teaching and learning resources across the campus has been positively addressed. The university has addressed future strategic developments including a programme of upgrading computer workstation clusters to cater for multimedia delivery, and network points are being provided in major teaching spaces. The Library has developed several major successful initiatives for digital archiving of important collections. It is also involved in several projects to improve access to electronic teaching and research resources, and to explore the potential of electronic publishing.

The Scholar Project, as our institutional TLTP project became known, took an holistic view of development across the whole university and was not driven by any one subject area. We always knew that in three years we would only be looking at the tip of the iceberg in terms of the impact we could make on teaching and learning at the university. The plan was to lay a basic foundation that we could build on for the future, and that would set a pattern of successful development and application of teaching material in the university curriculum.

Our approach was always to try to create an environment that enabled staff to naturally extend current preparation and teaching methods to incorporate the use of new technologies in a non-threatening way facilitated by a resource-based approach to development. We built upon existing small-scale activities in many different initiatives to develop computer-based teaching and learning materials that had arisen around the campus out of interest, and both internal and external funding. We sought to empower academic staff and departments to make use of multimedia technology while recognizing that not all staff would become 'multimedia authors'.

The project has demonstrated the need for two levels of ongoing support staff to enable a permanent and substantial shift of culture – authoring and technical. Such staff will work with both academic staff (subject teaching expertise) and central services (scanning, digitizing, video production, etc) to create the teaching material and make it available to the students. The ILC will not continue to expand by taking on more and more authoring staff. Rather, it will provide core services and support to enable departments to become self-sufficient in the development and delivery of computer-based teaching material.

Although not engaged in producing large suites of courseware, which was the remit of many subject-based consortia projects, Scholar was committed to producing resource-based learning materials working with a selection of academic departments. Projects were chosen on the basis of potential gains, which included providing alternative tutorials for large laboratory-based courses, enhancing and integrating information content of classes, dealing with conceptually difficult materials, and converting and enhancing resource-based learning delivery.

Details of early projects have been described elsewhere (Hutchings *et al.*, 1994; Hall *et al.*, 1995) and a comprehensive overview is currently being compiled within the Scholar Project final report. Through these activities the project sought to build up a strong internal network of staff with knowledge and expertise in the issues of integrating computer-based teaching and learning resources into traditional academic programmes.

Staff development

Staff development is essential in achieving change. For the Scholar Project it was also the means whereby the Interactive Learning Centre could come into contact with the greatest possible number of staff across the whole of the university. In the first year of activity approximately 20% of Southampton staff participated in ILC activities through a wide-ranging workshop and seminar programme dealing with generic issues of using and developing teaching and learning materials, and specific project development support in subject areas such as using Microcosm and evaluation. Three years on, demand has grown and staff training courses are now running at a level of at least three per week. Courses are routinely advertised through a blanket mail-out, with a reminder system in place to ensure attendance following booking. Such a high level of activity demands core financial support, which may be challenging in an economic climate where devolved budgets are the preferred funding model.

In the general context of a move to mainstream ILC activities, which was initiated by university management some 18 months into the project, these training workshops are now being developed in conjunction with the university-wide academic staff development programme, and the focus of teaching and learning issues is one stream to the new lecturer induction programme. However, it is useful to recognize that the staff development role of the centre is also embedded into the general advice and consultancy offered by the ILC to academics who seek to develop teaching and learning resources with support from the centre, and, as such, staff development is the responsibility of all ILC staff, whatever their special technical expertise. It is for this reason that the ILC, post TLTP funding, falls in the remit of Teaching Support and Media Services, which has sought to achieve synergy with its own pre-existing expertise placing Scholar Project activities within two activity streams of Educational Development and Multimedia Production.

Outcomes

The university has agreed to continue to core fund the Interactive Learning Centre as part of the strategic development of Teaching Support and Media Services although it will expect some income generation to offset central costs. As new technologies become mainstreamed, departments and faculties will be expected to pay more directly for ILC services. This is in keeping with the university's devolved funding framework in which there is minimum top slicing of funds in favour of a more market-oriented approach to the funding of academic and administrative support services through what is known as a 'core plus option' model.

The importance of the active support for the aims of the project by senior management in the university cannot be underestimated. Their support enabled us to establish the Scholar Project in the first instance and to take the first steps towards mainstreaming the activity as the project comes to an end. The university strategy document now contains the objective that by the year 2000, 20% of the students learning experience will be computer-based. It is the experience of the Scholar Project that has enabled the university to set such a bold objective, because that experience shows it is achievable through steady growth.

CONCLUSIONS

We have shown in the Scholar Project how important it is that an institution takes an holistic approach to the management of change involved in mainstreaming the use of new technology in teaching and learning. This includes the development of teaching and learning strategies at all levels (political, resource provision, curriculum design, etc), the development of institutional standards for the design and delivery of teaching material and staff development policies. It must be recognized that not all staff will become multimedia courseware authors – we don't all write textbooks after all. Rather we need new types of support staff, authoring and technical, who will work with academic staff to provide the teaching environment of the future. Such staff need not be additional to existing support staff, rather there should be a comprehensive plan for restructuring and retraining of staff to achieve the desired results.

Having said that all staff will not become multimedia authors, it is important that staff have a sense of 'ownership' of the material they will be using in their teaching. Hence the need for an institution to promote an incremental, resource-based approach to the development of such material. Resource material, which should be reusable for different teaching and learning needs, should be available for staff and students to access through digital libraries, whether campus or department/faculty based. Institutions will need to develop policies that enable access to material that it does not have copyright ownership of through the acquisition of network licences or whatever economic models evolve over the next few years. This will include negotiating access rights for staff and students to digital libraries held at other sites. A policy of staff development is essential to make staff aware of the implications of such developments.

We talked at the beginning of this paper about printed book becoming an everyday part of teaching and learning. Will the same be true for the use of technology in education? It is our belief that the development of the World Wide Web, which provides a user-friendly interface to all the material available on the Internet, together with the rapid developments in global communications is totally changing the way we perceive information and our ability to access it. Like many institutions, we have embraced this technology at Southampton, particularly because it helps promote the resource-based approach we describe above as well as providing a distributed method of access to network resources. We have developed a Web version of Microcosm, the Distributed Link Service, to explore the integration of these two technologies. This is being successfully applied in our eLIB project, the Open Journal Framework (Carr *et al.*, 1996, http://wwwcosm.ecs.soton.ac.uk/dls/).

Many people are discussing what the future holds for institutions of higher education but we do not want to get into the debate about the 'virtual university' here. However, it is safe to say that in the future our teaching methods will change, both as a result of political and funding changes and the technological revolution. There will be less face-to-face teaching, students will become much more autonomous in their learning patterns. There will be more electronic communication between students and staff, and students and students. We will have to address the methods by which we assess our students as the methodology changes. But, most importantly, staff and students will come to demand access to the network whenever and wherever they want it. We don't believe that throwing money into building new 'learning resource centres' is the answer. How can institutions afford to replace the technology at the rate at which it becomes obsolete these days? This model simply doesn't scale. New teaching methods that harness the enormous potential of new technology will only become effective when the ratio of students (and staff) to computers is one-to-one. We need to develop policies that enable all students to buy, lease or have access to their own portable computers which they can use to access resources on the network as an everyday occurrence.

Our final conclusion is that no member of staff can afford to ignore the changes that are taking place around them. Those who are reluctant or resistant can be encouraged to take those first steps towards the application of technology in their teaching by getting a networked machine on their desk, getting trained and starting to build their own electronic resource base, no matter if it is only identifying a few WWW sites that are relevant to their subject and starting to use them in their teaching. They won't even notice they've been hooked.

REFERENCES

Carr, L A, Davis, H C, Hall, W and Hey, J (1996) *Using the World Wide Web as an Electronic Library*, Proceedings of the ELVIRA (Electronic Libraries) Conference, Milton Keynes, April.

Davis, H C, Hall W, Heath, I, Hill, G and Wilkins, R (1992) 'Towards an Integrated Information Environment with Open Hypermedia Systems', in *ECHT '92: Proceedings of the Fourth ACM Conference on Hypertext*, ACM Press, pp.181–90

Hall, W, Davis, H C and Hutchings, G A (1996) *Rethinking Hypermedia: The Microcosm Approach*, Kluwer Academic Press.

Hall, W, Hutchings, G A and White, S A (1995) 'Breaking Down the Barriers: an Architecture for Developing and Delivering Resource-Based Learning Materials' in *Proceedings of the World Conference on Computers in Education*, Birmingham, England, July.

Hutchings G A, Hall, W and White, S (1994) 'Resource-Based Learning Using an Open Hypermedia System', Paper presented at Media Active, Liverpool.

Laurillard, D (1993) *Rethinking University Education: a Framework for the Effective Use of Technology*, Routledge, London.

McFarlane, A (1992) 'Teaching and Learning in an Expanding Higher Education System', The Committee of Scottish University Principals.

Mathias, H (1992) 'Survey of Computer Use in Teaching', University of Southampton.

Sprunt, B (1989) 'Interactive Video in Higher Education Project Report', University of Southampton.

Steinberg, S H (1955) 'Five Hundred Years of Printing', Penguin, Harmondsworth.

Woolf, B and Hall, W (1995) 'Multimedia Pedagogues: Interactive Systems for Teaching and Learning', *Computer*, **28**, 5, 74–80.

Chapter 4

Using Computer-Mediated Communication to Develop Supervisory Skills

Gerard Prendergast

INTRODUCTION

This chapter is a case study of a successful trial of the use of computer-mediated communication (CMC) for delivery of some forms of police training. I hope to draw some general conclusions on the issues of process, tutor's role, learning outcomes and evaluation. The aim of this chapter is also to answer some of the key questions associated with the use of computer-mediated communication for training purposes. It is intended to share the experiences gained in running the Gloucestershire Constabulary's Principles of Supervision Course, which was delivered by computer-mediated communication, asynchronously. This chapter also aims to give a better understanding of the CMC medium and its possible application in the workplace, for education or training purposes.

WHY FLEXIBLE LEARNING IS INCREASINGLY IMPORTANT IN THE POLICE SERVICE

The police service is having to adapt to a rapidly changing world. This has greatly increased the need for training, in order for the workforce to effectively cope with the effects of such change. The service faces a dichotomy over utilization of staff to meet ever-increasing operational demands and the need to have a properly trained staff. There is a growing recognition that we need to explore the potential of the new technologies that are becoming available to us, in order to cope effectively with some of these additional pressures, including:

- increased number of students;
- a more diverse subject area to cope with a more complex workload;

- increasing pressure on training staff;
- pressure from the public to have a more visible police presence;
- a realization of the benefits of teaching the concept of lifelong learning and the need to support it with effective flexible learning.

THE GLOUCESTERSHIRE CONSTABULARY COURSE

CMC training is a method of course delivery using computers, either with a modem or via a local area network. The system offers the possibility of training departments being able to increase the level of training while holding, or reducing, the rate of abstractions from the workplace. This is achieved by holding the training at, or near to, the workplace, or by students utilizing computers and modems in their homes.

Another advantage with this system is that it saves both the cost and time needed for travelling that conventional courses incur, bringing students together at a central location. This form of distance learning permits students to asynchronously access material 24 hours a day and get near-instant feedback.

The course had 21 students (four police sergeants, eight constables and nine civilian supervisors) who studied the Principles of Supervision. The aim of the first course run using this medium was to develop the students' knowledge and skills, as supervisors, or potential supervisors. The areas covered included:

- motivational theory;
- carrying out effective performance development reviews;
- developing staff;
- equal opportunities;
- evaluating staff progress;
- applying the disciplinary procedures (both police and civilian);
- stress management;
- problem solving.

Students all had a computer, a modem and a printer available in their homes. Most of the students borrowed this equipment from the Constabulary for the duration of the course. This pilot course was being run over a 24-week period, with students logging into a FirstClass conferencing system. A similar course commenced on 6 November, with 25 students (including two students from a neighbouring police force). The pilot course was evaluated by Ms Anita Pincas, a Senior Lecturer with the Institute of Education, London University.

Our course was hosted by the FirstClass conferencing system which is run by the European Police Information Centre (EPI-Centre). The EPI-Centre is housed at the Police Scientific Development Branch at Sandridge, Hertfordshire. We have a dedicated area on this system, called GLOSPOL TRAIN, which is a closed conference. This means that only nominated persons over whom I had control have access to this part of the system, and they accessed the course as it developed. I consider that this is essential to develop and maintain a safe learning environment.

Our students accessed the EPI-Centre from their homes using the public telephone system. The average cost was less than £5 per student per week and the Constabulary paid for this. This cash limit encourages the students to work, where possible, offline, by preparing their contributions for uploading prior to logging on. Students work from home, linking with fellow students and the tutor through both e-mail and computer conferencing, mostly studying at different times of the day.

This was particularly useful for the operational police officers, who work different shifts, as it permitted them to access material, and their fellow students, at their convenience. The students on the pilot course studied at home on average 8.5 hours per week, in their own time. Most police-run courses had previously been undertaken during duty time. Students were also required to complete a work-based project at the conclusion of the course. The project had to look at ways of enhancing their working environment.

The first module the students encountered was entitled 'Getting Started', which lasted a week. This module was designed to give students practice in communicating via CMC. It was also intended to expose them to working in small groups using the conferencing facility. The introductory exercise is shown in Figure 4.2.

Seventeen students successfully completed the course. Two students were badly injured while performing police duties (in separate unrelated incidents) and were unable to continue their studies. One student had to defer his studies, due to operational commitments (he is currently studying on the second course). One student felt the course was too demanding and withdrew at the end of the eighteenth week.

WHY EMPLOY COMPUTER-MEDIATED COMMUNICATION TO DELIVER TRAINING?

Linda Harasim (1992) describes online education as 'a unique combination of five factors: many-to-many communication, place independent, time independent, a text medium, and a computer-mediated medium.' Computer-mediated communication is a developing medium for educationand training. It has some advantages and disadvantages not found

Figure 4.1 *The EPI-CENTRE Desktop with GLOSPOL TRAIN open*

Monday, 24th April, 1995 09:19:44am

Getting Started Item
From: Gerard Prendergast
Subject: FIRST EXERCISE FOR TUTOR GROUPS
To: Getting Started

MY HOPES, FEARS and EXPECTATIONS.

Please discuss, with other members of your tutor group, the following:

(a) What you hope to gain from this course?
(b) What fears do you have about your involvement in this course? and
(c) What do you expect to gain from the course and the tutors?

You will need, as a group to post a summary of your conclusions to the main 'Getting Started' conference. This should be completed by Sunday 30 April 1995.

Figure 4.2 *Introductory exercise*

together in other forms of course delivery. As it uses both the computer e-mail and conferencing systems, it offers:

- One-to-one communication (e-mail: tutor/student or student/student). This is useful to the tutor for giving advice and praise where it would be inappropriate to have an audience, and it allows students to air problems confidentially, with both tutors and peers.
- One-to-many (conference: tutor/students or student/students).
- Many-to-many (conference: tutors/students/students, in any combination). This permits groupwork to take place and real 'process' is often experienced. I have found that there is a much more even level of contribution from the participants than in a conventional class.

Dr Robin Mason (1991) suggests:

'Computer conferencing above all forms of computer networking, is a hybrid, uniting the social function of spoken communication with the logical and textual qualities of written communication.'

Both forms of communication skills are extremely important, in the police service.

Some of the benefits

Users of CMC for education or training have found that students participate more fully, often taking the learning process beyond that originally intended by the course designers. This was reflected on the pilot course by our students. An example of this can be seen in a weekly report reproduced in Figure 4.3.

'Friday, June 16, 1995 07:44:33pm
Message
From: XXXX YYYYY
Subject: Progress Report Week 8
To: Gerard Prendergast

---

what a week!
I would not be exaggerating if I said I had put in over 25 hours this week,
but that was due to 2 very fragmented weeks preceding.
I was almost disturbed by the fact that having joined the [Public] * library
and taken out 5 books I found myself actually enjoying them, especially as it
all made sense with the knowledge gain from the course so far. Had I read
the books before the course I would have found them heavy going.
Wednesday was...

Have fun reading the essays.
Mark.
(Added by me for clarification)

Figure 4.3 *Example weekly report*

Morten Soby (1992) maintains

> 'The popularity of the electronic socialising form leaves no doubt that participation in conferences has a beneficial effect on motivation. There is evidence indicating a positive relationship between participation in conferences and course completion or success in the final examination. The importance of the social dimension of computer-mediated communication should not be overlooked. Students get a sense of belonging as a result of participation.'

There is generally a higher level of mutual support among students and tutors. On many occasions, when students expressed a lack of understanding of a concept or issue, other students offered explanations and help. Jesus Rueda (1992) acknowledges similar findings when he wrote 'they develop strong links that enable them to support each other and engage in extra work, to supply solutions to other peoples' problems.'

There appears to be an enhancement of the tutors' teaching role, because of the increased willingness of the students to collaborate with their peers and the tutors in the learning process. This encouraged me to give something extra, as a tutor.

Due to the asynchronous nature of this medium, team teaching by tutors is much easier to accommodate. The inclusion of input from people with subject expertise, but no teaching skills, is a benefit, provided that trained tutor support is available.

This form of distance learning is free of time and place constraints and offers near-instant feedback to students, often not available with other forms of distance learning. This is of a particular benefit to organizations, such as the police, because of the need to have staff operating 24 hours a day.

The 'little and often' nature of this study medium means that retention levels of knowledge are often higher.

There is a more even distribution of student contribution than in a normal classroom environment. This system encourages reflective thought and therefore assists the normally less extrovert student to participate more fully. This was stated very clearly by one of the students when she posted the following extract shown in Figure 4.4.

'*Tuesday, June 13, 1995 08:46:32pm*
Online Training Item
From: XXXXXX YYYYYY
Subject: emma re course
To: Online Training
*Emma I was interested to see your comments. I have been a supervisor for
some years now, but I feel more confident now, even though we have only
completed one module. In a classroom I would find, especially after lunch,
that my mind would wander off. You can take only so much in at a time.
With this method of learning I feel that I am appreciating the theories more
than I would in the classroom. I can work at my pace, when I want. I can
take my time digesting them.* **I am contributing more, as in a classroom
there is always one who has an opinion on everything. I tend to keep
quiet. The present course is a great leveller as far as contribution is
concerned.**
*There are downsides of course. A lot of time spent typing, but I must admit
my keyboard skills have improved. Also our time is being used rather than
the firms, but we are getting a lot out of it personally as well.
I volunteered for the course as much as to gain experience with using
computers, and I feel that I'm not frightened of them anymore. It's harder
work than I thought but I'm getting a tremendous amount out of it. I don't
know what I will do in the evenings when the course is finished, I'm hooked.
I may even have to get my own modem.*'

Figure 4.4 *Student extract*

Trevor Owen (1991) considers that:

'Asynchronous communication is, in my view, essentially reflective and
responsive communication. And this asynchronous nature suggests the
possibility of dealing with online material in a variety of ways that are capable
of promoting and sustaining considered response within a textual community.
Capturing, or downloading the electronic text for reading off-line, or in printed
form, for instance, is something we encourage our students to do so that they
may feel free to contribute in whatever ways they find appropriate – and at
times when they feel it is appropriate as well. I believe this happens best when
people have had a chance to reflect on their experience, consider the language
they would choose to express their ideas, and compose their ideas to their
own satisfaction.'

I have found that my students have behaved in this way.

An added bonus is that students gain some computer skills. About 70%
of our students, on the pilot course had little or no computer experience,
prior to the start of this course. They now feel comfortable using their
machines.

Another benefit of this training is that students become comfortable and
proficient with the use of e-mail and have the ability to utilize computer
communication to access and share information.

Some disadvantages

There is an initial learning curve for students, who are unfamiliar with computers or computer conferencing. However the FirstClass conferencing system (as used by EPI-Centre) has a fairly shallow learning curve. This is very important for the non-computer user. Most of the students appeared to be able to cope after about one hour of instruction. Once they knew how to log-on, log-off and upload a message, further instruction was delivered via CMC, thus enhancing their ability to utilize the systems and benefit from it. We are continuing to try to improve on this area of our training. The ease of use was summed up by another student, as illustrated in Figure 4.5.

> 'When I enrolled on to this course, I felt I had very little experience of computer technology, however I was soon to realize that some of my fellow students had never switched 'the box' on – My first lesson, if they were willing to try so was I. My first task was to discuss my hopes, fears and expectations of the course, how reassuring to discover others felt the same way. What really fascinated me was how quickly I was to become an EPI-CENTRE Junkie and how my thoughts differed from those of other people. By reading fellow students' inputs I soon discovered how my own thoughts could be challenged, how I could enlighten my views and broaden my horizons by 'mulling over' other peoples opinions. Now one month into the course I have discovered that the learning process of any subject is addictive and just as the body of an athlete strives for the adrenaline 'fix' in sport so the brain craves for further education. By adopting this way of learning, we remove the pressures, after all if we want a night off, we just don't switch 'the box' on. However, I put money on the chance of me not coming home and logging on to see if anyone's talking to me !'

Figure 4.5 *Student response extract*

There can be technical difficulties to overcome, but these are diminishing with the latest software. By supplying preconfigured, tested computers we have managed to reduce such difficulties greatly.

Initial set-up costs, both for hardware and software, need to be considered. Again, both hardware and software costs are decreasing. Many employees already own or are contemplating buying their own machines, for home use. Gloucestershire Constabulary has spent £20,000 on equipment, which is less than the cost of supplying and equipping a conventional classroom. A grant of £5,000, towards our costs was generously donated by the Gloucestershire Training Enterprise Council. These costs do not include the host software.

This medium has a real telepresence and it takes a few weeks for most students/tutors to adapt to the difference in the communication style of CMC. Anita Pincas (1995) has found that: 'students normally adapt to it [CMC] almost at once. It seems that the innate human ability to communicate will easily compensate for any initial difficulties due to the new medium.'

Time management can be problematic for both student and tutors. They may need to spend more time managing this aspect. Students on the Principles of Supervision course believe that their time-management skills had dramatically improved by the end of the course. This helped with students' confidence in their ability to learn.

Some 14 students have indicated that they have enrolled or intend enrolling in part-time courses in further or higher education, citing their experience on the Principles of Supervision course as the spur. The textual nature of the interactions may also create a greater level of confidence. Ong (1982) considers: 'Writing introduces division and alienation, but a higher unity as well. It intensifies the sense of self and fosters more conscious interaction between persons. Writing is consciousness-raising.'

Due to the higher levels of student (and sometimes tutor) participation, information overload can cause difficulties. This needs careful management by the course leader.

CAN PROCESS TAKE PLACE ON COMPUTER-MEDIATED COMMUNICATION?

'CMC systems must provide an environment which people find personally motivating and enjoyable to enter, which allows the magic of CMC to occur. Once the initial familiarisation phase is over, it is important that the design of the system encourages feelings of "groupness" and "telepresence" encouraging users to identify with other members of their group, despite constraints of time and space' (Kaye, 1992).

I believe this is a very important aspect of CMC and with this in mind I designed my course.

In order to foster 'groupness', I started the course with a face-to-face one-day meeting. The aim of the day was to get students to meet, mix and get to know (to some extent) as many of their fellow students as possible. Various small group tasks were undertaken where students were required to works with different colleagues. Tasks included:

- deciding what should be included in their online resumés;
- designing an heraldic shield that showed each person's past, greatest regret, greatest achievement and future hopes;
- explaining the shields to each other; and
- exploring, in groups of five, the CMC facility and then undertaking a presentation of their 'discoveries'.

I have now held two introductory meetings (one for the pilot course and one for the present course) and both courses resulted in the students reaching at least the first of the forming, storming, norming and performing stages of group development. Such introductions also helped to introduce students to a different style of learning, as many of the students had been used to a purely didactic style of course delivery. Police training in more recent years has favoured more of a facilitative approach. Students were also appraised of the likely workload involved (in the event, they insisted on completing more than they were asked to do!) I believe that the seeds of real learning communities were sown at the introductory face-to-face meetings. These learning communities fostered the idea that they were responsible for managing their own learning (the depth, effort and involvement, at least to some extent) and for helping and encouraging others within their tutor group.

Anita Pincas (1995) states in her report: 'a dialogue-based process like CMC allows learners to direct their own enquiry to a considerable extent along lines that flow from their initial conceptualizations'.

This was articulated by one of the students commenting on the course, as shown in Figure 4.6.

Later instances of supportive and corrective feedback were practised and accepted, in such groups using the CMC medium. This whole process, I believe, greatly assisted the students to start and develop the process of 'collaborative learning'. John Grundy (1992) and his colleagues defined collaborative learning as 'individual learning as a result of group process'. He goes on to explain:

> 'At its heart it is the process by which people learn as a result of interactions with their peers. It is important to recognize the contrast between the collaborative learning model and the transmissive model of traditional formal education, in which interactions occur principally between the teacher and the student.'

While many of the students are seeking promotion (which is competitive), they readily shared their knowledge and worked in a very collaborative way. This experience may have a long-term effect on the organization as it showed the benefits of active collaboration by multidisciplinary teams. Such teams were present as course tutor groups. One student stated in his post course evaluation 'In a classroom situation there is always the one or two [students] who dominate the discussions. It is more difficult to do so through the Net, and everyone's contribution has equal value'. Grundy summed this up, succinctly: 'It seems that a barrier to achieving team-based work organizations is people's socialization by competitive, individualistic educational environment.'

To enhance such collaborative learning, I believe that it is important that students are encouraged to be active participants and not just lurkers. The term 'lurker' denotes a person who reads the contributions submitted by fellow students, but does not make an active contribution. This is where the size of the tutor group, I believe, is crucial. Small groups have a psychological effect on the participants and make them much more likely

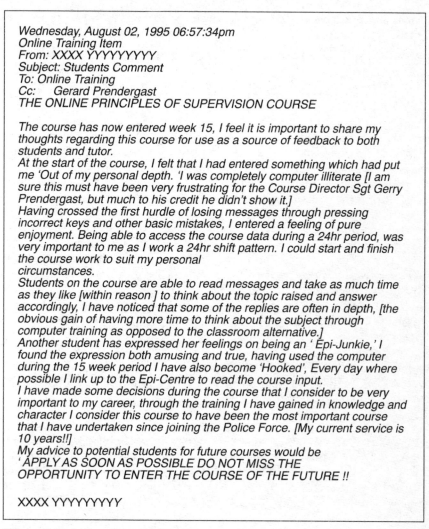

Wednesday, August 02, 1995 06:57:34pm
Online Training Item
From: XXXX YYYYYYYYY
Subject: Students Comment
To: Online Training
Cc: Gerard Prendergast
THE ONLINE PRINCIPLES OF SUPERVISION COURSE

The course has now entered week 15, I feel it is important to share my thoughts regarding this course for use as a source of feedback to both students and tutor.
At the start of the course, I felt that I had entered something which had put me 'Out of my personal depth.' I was completely computer illiterate [I am sure this must have been very frustrating for the Course Director Sgt Gerry Prendergast, but much to his credit he didn't show it.]
Having crossed the first hurdle of losing messages through pressing incorrect keys and other basic mistakes, I entered a feeling of pure enjoyment. Being able to access the course data during a 24hr period, was very important to me as I work a 24hr shift pattern. I could start and finish the course work to suit my personal circumstances.
Students on the course are able to read messages and take as much time as they like [within reason] to think about the topic raised and answer accordingly, I have noticed that some of the replies are often in depth, [the obvious gain of having more time to think about the subject through computer training as opposed to the classroom alternative.]
Another student has expressed her feelings on being an ' Epi-Junkie,' I found the expression both amusing and true, having used the computer during the 15 week period I have also become 'Hooked', Every day where possible I link up to the Epi-Centre to read the course input.
I have made some decisions during the course that I consider to be very important to my career, through the training I have gained in knowledge and character I consider this course to have been the most important course that I have undertaken since joining the Police Force. [My current service is 10 years!!]
My advice to potential students for future courses would be
'APPLY AS SOON AS POSSIBLE DO NOT MISS THE OPPORTUNITY TO ENTER THE COURSE OF THE FUTURE !!

XXXX YYYYYYYYY

Figure 4.6 *Student's comments on the course*

to make contributions. Such groups also help to prevent information overload, which can be a real problem for participants using computer-mediated communication. Having experimented with various group sizes, I have found that five students per tutor group is the optimum. With more than six, I have noticed that there is a tendency for at least one student to become a lurker. Less than four tends to reduce the benefits of collaborative learning and greatly restricts the cross-fertilization of ideas. The amount of messages generated by active individuals in a group larger than six tends to make it hard for the individuals to keep in touch with the subjects under discussion. Students also recognized the importance of the tutor group size. One student made the following point in his post course evaluation:

'Discussions need to be within the tutor group, otherwise its gets unwieldy. Early on in the course a couple of discussions went on in the open forum, and because of the time delay element, lost direction. The policy seemed to have altered during the course, and may have changed just for that reason.'

Each small group task was lead by one of the students within the tutor group. The designated student was assigned the role of group summarizer and had to prepare and post the group findings to the plenary area, so that other groups could read, compare and comment on the findings of the course as a whole. Each student had to perform the summarizer's task more than once during the course. This ensured that each group has a student who encouraged participation by the other members of the group. This rotation of responsibility also allowed each student to practice collating and summarizing information from different sources. Occasionally, it also required skills of reconciliation to be employed, so that a consensus summary could be posted. By reading the various group summaries, I was able to ensure that students had gained a good understanding of the issues involved, and correct any misconceptions that might have arisen. The students, by reading the other groups' summaries, were also reinforcing their knowledge.

WHAT IS THE TUTOR'S ROLE IN DELIVERING A COURSE USING CMC?

I believe that in order to be an effective online tutor (a tutor who employs CMC), a person needs the same skills as a conventional tutor. One of the most difficult tasks is trying to achieve the balance between guiding the student's work and encouraging them to be responsible for their own learning, in their own way. In attempting to achieve such a balance a tutor needs to:

- keep the students' workloads to manageable levels (information overload is a potential problem in all CMC delivered courses);
- motivate the students by stimulating their interest;
- give supportive and corrective feedback in a style that is appropriate to the individual;
- develop a sufficiently relaxed atmosphere to make the learning experience both pleasant and valuable;
- maintain the tutor's authority while conveying understanding and empathy.

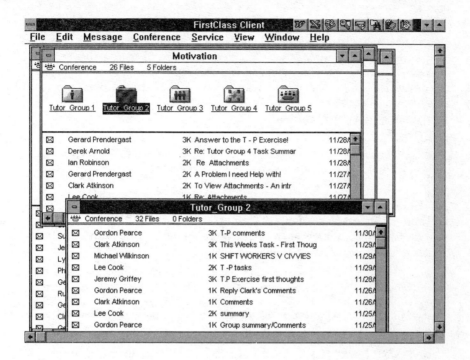

Figure 4.7 *Tutor groups set up in the FirstClass system*

Being such a paragon of virtue is not enough, in my view, to be a good online tutor. While the need to have these attributes (at least to some degree) is essential, there are some additional skills necessary to be effective in this role. Derek Rowntree (1990) points out:

> 'Teachers who teach well face-to-face are not necessarily so proficient at teaching through written comments, where they cannot see the student's reaction to what they have said and so amend it accordingly.'

The ability to express oneself clearly in the written medium is an essential requirement. It helps if such written expression conveys the supporting emotions, such as empathy, understanding and humour. Like all skills, written skills improve with practice. Another problem is the dual role that an online tutor has to come to terms with. This is explained by David McConnell (1992):

> 'We are constantly confronted with the contradiction in playing the dual role of tutor–participant. This is especially so in the assessment process. Any intervention we make has the likelihood of being received differently to interventions made by other participants.'

I have found that when my students expanded the learning beyond the boundaries that I had envisaged (a regular occurrence), I was very strongly tempted to become an active participant in the resulting discussions. McConnell's observations ensured that I was extremely careful not to stifle or guide by an ill-conceived interjection. This does not mean that intervention is not required – it is a question of judgement and degree. Christina Simon (1992) contends:

> 'Successful experiences of peer collaboration tell us that the tutor has to make group members aware of the fact that their own experiences are relevant and worth telling to the group, and that other peers are as valuable a source of knowledge as the rest of the components in the course.'

As with face-to-face education or training, the purpose of the activity, the age and ability of the students and the entry level of students' knowledge will dictate (to some degree at least) the role taken by the tutor. Anthony Kaye (1992) recognized this when he wrote:

> 'When this person is a teacher, and the evaluator of the participant's works and inputs, a different style of interaction is likely to develop from a seminar or syndicate situation, in which each member of the group has knowledge and skills to share with others, and the leader's role is more that of a facilitator and resource person, as well as being a peer.'

I believe that I have found a very successful way of tutoring, that is right for me and the students that I deal with. I am conscious that there will be other modes of online tutoring that will be equally successful for other personalities and other types of courses. Having said that, the very nature of the CMC medium tends to favour the syndicate-based learning and this type of approach appears to be responsible for the increased collaborate learning that many educators have observed. We will be experimenting with the use CMC in other areas.

Dr Robin Mason (1991), talking about a conference moderator's role, thinks that it should combine 'elements of teacher, chairman, host, facilitator and community organizer'. I consider that the online tutor also requires these elements to be successful. There is also a need for online tutors to be able to exercise a different form of control, due to the asynchronous nature of the medium. This was recognized by Anthony Kaye (1992):

> 'The fact that computer conferencing allows collaboration to progress without the need for set places and times for meetings and other highly visible decision-points does not mean that there should be no rhythm or pacing of conferencing discussions.'

An advantage the online tutor has over his face-to-face colleague is time to reflect on when and how to intervene, again due to the time-independent nature of the medium.

An online tutor will also need to 'netweave'. Netweaving is the ability to summarize the state of the various discussions to locate and point out the various threads of unity in the comments of the students and tutor(s). This is not always easy, as the fertile imagination of the human brain will often result in a written submission dealing with a number of different issues, which have previously been raised, under the one message heading. I found that my ability to netweave improved dramatically with regular monitoring of the students' inputs to the course.

If this all appears to be daunting, the practice, for me anyway, has been one of the most rewarding experiences that I have ever had. I have seen, and been able to track the real progress made by my students. The medium makes this possible because of the semi-permanent nature of the written contributions. Not only have I the ability to see such progress, but I can also point this out to each student and refer them to their early contributions and get them to compare such contributions with their present written assertions.

I spent between one and two hours each day (including weekends) reading the various student contributions and writing replies. Such tasks were often dealt with over half hour periods. I found the 'little and often' approach to tutoring more productive. I also spent time on the pastoral care and on creating and maintaining hardcopy student files, which were of immense benefit for keeping track of the level of a particular student's involvement. Marking of the various module assignments, such as the essay entitled 'What influences motivation?' (which was required at the end of the Motivation module), required about one hour for each student (21 hours at the end of each module, on the pilot course). In addition to this, time was required for the preparation of course material and the occasional ad hoc telephone or face-to-face tutorials. I estimate that I spend about 16 hours a week on tutoring this course.

WHAT LEARNING OUTCOMES CAN TRAINING USING CMC DELIVER?

The learning outcomes of most courses run using an element of CMC will be strongly influenced by the degree of collaborative learning that has taken place. The quality of collaborative learning will depend on the quality of the students who take an active part in the course. Another variable affecting collaborative learning is what is being learned or developed and the way that the course is structured. Sarah Kiesler (1992) maintains:

> 'in collaborative learning, people learn from one another, more than when one person is talking. Also in collaborative learning, learners are teachers, and teachers, learners. Talking, teaching, and learning are intertwined processes in groups.'

In CMC, talking is replaced by the written word. Anita Pincas (1995) found that my students were impressed with the CMC medium and had great expectations of this medium. Quoting her findings:

> 'The majority felt very positive about the prospect of working closely with other students, even at a distance, and expected to learn a lot from each other, even though 12 considered themselves reserved or shy in traditional seminars.'

The students' expectations appear to have been met, on the whole. In weekly reports and in the end of course questionnaires, students mentioned learning most when 'we spent a lot of time discussing the issues and ensuring they had sunk in!'

A face-to-face meeting was held at the end of the course. The purpose of this day was to permit students to meet with the external evaluator (Anita Pincas) and to have the opportunity to take part in face-to-face tutorials. It was also used to allow the students the time to consider just what they had gained from the course. They were sent away, in four groups, to consider that issue. They were unsupervised, except for random visits by the external evaluator. They produced flipcharts of what they considered were their learning outcomes. They then amalgamated their findings and produced the list shown in Figure 4.8 (my comments on their findings). I am not claiming that all of these learning outcomes were necessarily achieved. This was the perception of the students on the course.

HOW CAN WE EVALUATE THE USE OF CMC FOR TRAINING?

I believe that the computer-mediated communication is an excellent medium for assessing a great number of skills and attributes that it might be desirable for students to acquire. The semi-permanent (electronic) or permanent (hardcopy) record of a student's contributions is easy to access and review, at any time during or after the course. In a face-to-face situation, unless each session is recorded (either audio or video) the students' verbal contributions and group interactions cannot be examined in detail and, at best, a general impression of such interactions is all that can be obtained.

The evaluation of the Principles of Supervision course was undertaken in three parts:

1. An independent evaluation by Ms Pincas of the Institute of Education, London University.

2. A week-by-week ongoing evaluation by the tutor, using the students weekly reports and assessment of groupwork at the end of each week.

3. An end of course assessment on each student, which relied heavily on the student's various assignments and his or her contributions, both in quality and quantity during the life of the course.

SUPERVISORY SKILLS
Indepth understanding of the supervisor's role, actions and their effects
Understanding of management attitudes and styles
Understanding of theory behind behaviour
Change in attitude and working practices *(the students')*
(The way they approached their roles of supervision had been strongly influenced by their studies)

PERSONAL SKILLS
Computer familiarization
(It introduced many of them to the benefits of using a computer)
Typing practice
(Such skills improved through use!)
Essay writing practice
(Some of the assignments were of the essay variety)
Developing a project and writing a project report
(Their individual project developed skills of research, information retrieval, collation and written presentation)

PERSONAL DEVELOPMENT
Build confidence – overcome fear of stating own views
(Some of the students felt that their confidence has grown considerably and that they now realized that their opinions were value.)
Broaden horizons – eye opener
(The interaction via the computer gave everyone a much greater appreciation of the functions and responsibilities of other Constabulary's employees)
Improve interpersonal skills
(The students stated that in real terms, there is more interaction online. People who are normally shy and quiet contributed much more than in a face-to-face situation).
Time management – Discipline – Planning
(As the students were studying in their own time they were forced to plan and manage their time effectively in order to cope with the course and their other responsibilities.).
Self Motivation
(Many students intend enrolling on other part-time adult education courses as a direct result of their experience and motivation resulting from studying on this course)
Sense of accomplishment
(Students who completed the course found it interesting and rewarding. They stated that they had worked hard and had gained a real sense of achievement)

OTHER BENEFITS
Extensive contact with a wide range of Individuals – Cross fertilization
Development of a team spirit – CMC level communications
(Students developed a real team spirit while working in their tutor groups).
Integration of Police and Civilian Support Staff
Motivation Module very useful for the Police Promotion assessment system
Gets people back into learning

Figure 4.8 *Summary of students' responses to the course*

The independent evaluation

The independent evaluator considered whether CMC-delivered training was a suitable vehicle for police training of full-time working staff. She looked at whether the students perceived the benefits of firstly the course content and secondly the online training method. She also thought carefully about whether the students were able to study collaboratively at a distance with each other while working full-time. She considered whether students appreciated the online method of working collaboratively with fellow students and their tutor. The evaluator wished to know whether such an online course could be managed by other trainers. Lastly, she wished to determine whether the course could provide a model for police training generally, and to recommend how this might be accomplished.

The evaluation was carried out by Ms Pincas employing pre- and post-course student questionnaires. She also attended both face-to-face days (initial and final course meeting) where she met, talked to and observed both students and tutor in groups and privately. She had continuous access to all of the course material (paper, video and online) and was able to question the tutor as to the intended learning outcomes. She regularly read the various contributions during the life of the course. Lastly she was sent a copy of each student's weekly learning report.

In the summary of her findings she states that the overall result is a very positive one:

'The students have enjoyed the course and felt that it has been of considerable educational benefit to them. They have also made numerous useful suggestions… There is no doubt that this course could become a general model of in-service training.'

Ms Pincas made a number of recommendations, some of which have already been implemented on the second Principles of Supervision course, and the remainder will be implemented in the future.

The week-by-week ongoing evaluation

I used the results of groupwork as part of the evaluation because it tends to show the student's willingness to cooperate with their peers, which is very relevant to many work situations, especially within the police service. It also gave a very good indication of the level of understanding reached by the students on the subject being studied, and their level of commitment to the course. The ability to check just what each student had read and/or commented on (a feature of the FirstClass conferencing system) also enabled me to see the level of interest that various group exercises generated.

I think that most pertinent evaluation issues, as far as CMC is concerned, relate to what can be done with this medium that could not be done before (in traditional educational delivery). For example, in groupwork and group

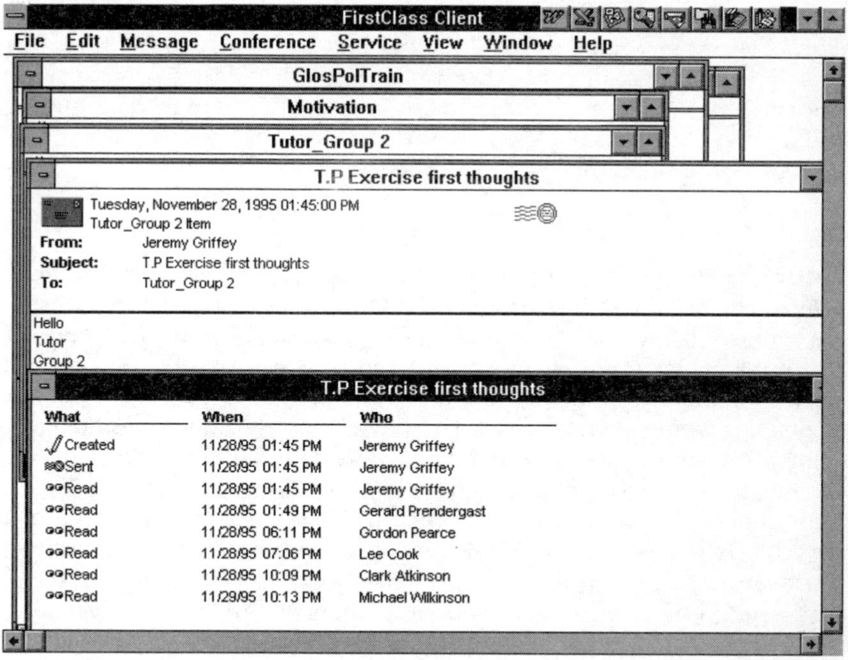

Figure 4.9 *Determining who has read and/or commented on a message (a feature of the FirstClass conferencing system)*

assessments, I can see just who is contributing and who is not. I can check the level of interest in the task and stimulate additional interest by interjecting or advancing a hypothesis. I could have reconstructed an entire tutor group's interaction, either electronically or in hardcopy, by calling up the recorded responses of the participants.

Students were obliged to submit a weekly report (by midnight on Sunday night). This was used as another tool in my ongoing evaluation. Students had to report on the following areas:

1. What learning did they think they achieved during the preceding week and what use did they think such learning might be? How did they feel about what they had learned?

2. What problems did they have (if any) that impinged on their study, in the preceding week? These could be of a work, personal or technical nature? I did not expect any details of personal problems, just an awareness that a student was having some (general) social difficulty.

3. What was likely to get in the way of learning in the forthcoming week, such as annual leave, attendance at court or a residential training course?

Students were, in effect, maintaining a form of electronic learning diary when they were completing the first section of their report, which was accessible to the tutor. Such reports, especially when they contained the students' thoughts and feelings, were invaluable to me in determining whether or not intervention was required. I was able to adjust the course content as a result of this ongoing feedback.

End of course assessment on each student

I kept a hardcopy file on each course participant. This folder contained a printed copy of anything meaningful that the student contributed during the course. This included the written assignments. With the exception of the final project report, every written assignment was submitted electronically. The tutor-marked assignments, containing the feedback comments, were returned via the computer and modem to the student. A summative report was produced on each student and forwarded to their Commander or Department Head, after having been discussed with the individual concerned at the end-of-course evaluation day. I found it particularly useful to be able to review contributions that the student had made throughout the course in completing these reports. It enabled me to see the progress made by the individual comparing the quality of their earlier submissions to that of the latter contributions. I was able to evidence all my remarks by referencing to such material.

The level of evaluation that Anita Pincas and I were able to undertake was much more comprehensive than anything we could have achieved in a conventional course, with the same amount of effort.

CONCLUSIONS

This form of training offers another tool for training delivers. I consider that the full potential of this medium has not yet been developed. I believe that we are currently at the stage of development with this medium that the early cinema photographers reached when the cine-camera was first invented. They started by filming plays and then developed the art of producing films, which fully exploited that medium. With constant use and experimentation, I foresee that a unique type of course will evolve that will fully exploit the benefits of CMC. Until we develop such a course, I will continue to employ a 'mix and match' approach with CMC, using a combination of delivery tools to try to gain the maximum benefit for students.

The pilot course run by the Gloucestershire Constabulary was considered to be a success, by the students, tutor, independent evaluator and the Force Training Officer. As a result of this, the second course is currently being held and various different courses are now being planned for future delivery by this exciting medium. A number of other UK police forces and government departments, having seen the Gloucestershire experiment, are now planning to introduce training that employs this medium.

Acknowledgements

The inspiration for introducing computer-mediated communication into Training in the Gloucestershire Constabulary, was my study undertaken on the postgraduate 'Online Education and Training' course, which was delivered by Anita Pincas, Dr Robin Mason, Anthony R Kaye and Laury Melton at the Institute of Education, London University, in 1994. I am also privileged to be a visiting tutor on the 1996 OET course.

Many of my experiences as an online tutor were gained as a visiting tutor on the Open University's 'Teaching and Learning Online' courses which Derek Rowntree, Professor of Educational Development, Open University, has been kind enough to invite me to partake in since 1994.

REFERENCES

Grundy, J (1992) 'Understanding Collaborative Learning in Networked Organisations', in *Collaborative Learning Through Computer Conferencing: The Najaden Papers*, A R Kaye (ed.), Springer-Verlag, Berlin.

Hart, John, E (forthcoming) 'Computer Conferencing in an MA in Information Technology', in *Improving the Quality of Teaching and Learning in Computing Vol. 2*, Staff and Educational Development Association (SEDA), Birmingham.

Harasim, L (1992) 'Online Education: An Environment for Learning and Intellectual Amplification' in *Online Education*, L Harasim (ed.), New York Press, NY.

Kaye, A R (1992) 'Learning Together Apart', in *Collaborative Learning Through Computer Conferencing: The Najaden Papers*, A R Kaye (ed.), Springer-Verlag, Berlin.

Kiesler, S (1992) 'Talking, Teaching and Learning in Network Groups', in *Collaborative Learning Through Computer Conferencing: The Najaden Papers*, A R Kaye (ed.), Springer-Verlag, Berlin.

Mason, R (1991) 'The Textuality of Computer Networking', in *Computer Conferencing The Last Word...*, R Mason (ed.), Beach Holme Publishers Ltd, Victoria, British Columbia.

McConnell, D (1992) 'Computer Mediated Communication for Management Learning', in *Collaborative Learning Through Computer Conferencing: The Najaden Papers*, A R Kaye (ed.), Springer-Verlag, Berlin.

Mason, R D (1991) 'Moderating Educational Conferencing', *DEOSNEWS*, 1, 1, Pennsylvania State University.

O'Hagan, C (1995a) 'Views of Learning, Based on the Experience of Running Computer Conferencing Courses', in *Empowering Learners and Teachers Through Technology*, C O'Hagan (ed.), Publication No. 90, SEDA, Birmingham.

O'Hagan, C (1995b) 'Analysis of Face to Face and Computer Conferencing Interactions in University Teaching', in *Empowering Learners and Teachers Through Technology*, C O'Hagan (ed.), Publication No. 90, SEDA, Birmingham.

Owen, T (1991) 'Wired Writing: The Writers in Electronic Residence Program', in *Computer Conferencing The Last Word…* R Mason (ed.), Beach Holme Publishers Ltd, Victoria, British Columbia.

Ong, W (1982) *Orality and Literacy: The Technologizing of the Word*, Methuen, London and New York.

Pincas, A (1995) Independent Evaluation Report on 'The Online Principles of Supervision' course, Gloucestershire Constabulary Training Department, Section 2.4.2 ii, Institute of Education, London University.

Rueda, J (1992) 'Collaborative Learning in a Large Scale Computer Conferencing System', in *Collaborative Learning Through Computer Conferencing: The Najaden Papers*, A R Kaye (ed.), Springer-Verlag, Berlin.

Rowntree, D (1990) *Developing Courses for Students*, McGraw-Hill, London.

Soby, M (1992) 'Waiting for Electropolis', in *Collaborative Learning Through Computer Conferencing: The Najaden Papers*, A R Kaye (ed.), Springer-Verlag, Berlin.

Simon, C (1992) 'Telematic Support for In-Service Teacher Training', in *Collaborative Learning Through Computer Conferencing: The Najaden Papers*, A R Kaye (ed.), Springer-Verlag, Berlin.

Chapter 5

Technology *in* Education to Technology *of* Education: Concepts, Conflicts and Compromises

Ray McAleese

OVERVIEW

This chapter overviews the contribution that instructional technology has played in the development of learning environments. These events are used to suggest the likely changes required by staff and students in higher education if they are to make the most of the current technology rich system. After reviewing the range of instructional theories, I assess the contribution of instructional technology or a technology *of* education. A starting point is to consider the current focus on technology *in* education. I argue that this emphasis is misplaced as it concentrates on the artefacts of education, rather than addressing the way learners can come to know. The implications for developing staff and appropriate structures to support teachers and learners are drawn out at the end of the chapter.

A PROMISE UNFULFILLED?

Some 30 years ago, when the Association for Programmed Learning was founded, the first issue of its journal carried a message from the Minister of Education, Sir Edward Boyle. He wrote, 'Many experiments are taking place in the writing of programs and in the use of teaching machines, and I am sure that there are promising developments ahead' (*Programmed Learning*, 1964). In the Editorial, the Editor John Annett (who went on to a distinguished career in education) writing again of the potential for innovative experiments in educational technology, observed:

> 'Many of these attempts have been dramatically successful... Different methods reflect different views on the underlying psychological and educational theory, but there is a fundamental unity in this diversity – *namely*

to put teaching on a firmly scientific basis and from this to develop a new technology adequate to meet the rapidly growing demand for training and education.' [my emphasis] (*Programmed Learning*, 1964)

The halcyon days of the 1960s seems a far cry from the apparent reality of teaching in the 1990s. The potential for a technology *of* education[1] seems to have been wasted in pursuit of a technology *in* education. The developments in different approaches to teaching in schools, further and higher education have been largely as a result of the microchip or some other form of technical artefact. I want to explore why this has come about and to suggest that there is no inevitability in this movement. In a recent review of factors that influence the adoption of instructional design in the USA (Cummings, 1995), the author suggests that a lack of firm knowledge of instructional technology and hard wired theories of teaching and learning have been most influential. I am going to describe a technology *of* education, or what is better known as 'educational technology', in terms of a cybernetic system involving learners, teachers, ideas and support for learning. To begin with, we should be aware of the current battleground.

THE PRESENT CONTEXT

In response to the announcement of the Dearing Review, the *Times Higher Education Supplement* has been carrying articles from major thinkers in education and information technology. Seeley Brown and Duiguid (1996) make an incisive point. They say, 'the idea of the virtual university... both under-estimates how universities as institutions work *and over-estimates what communications technologies can do.'* They go on to suggest that communications technologies can and do support and transform educational interactions. Yet they leave the reader in no doubt that the technology alone has not been the significant driver for change. They identify the social and structural changes that have taken place as important contributors. The idea of what drives change is a useful idea for our thinking. I am certain that most stakeholders in education (eg, parents, teachers, politicians) would identify computer-based technology as a major agent for change. They might not agree on its positive benefits, but there is ample evidence for them to draw on to support this claim. The National Council for Educational Technology published an important monograph in 1994 called *IT Works*. In this they set out a number of assertions and supporting evidence on the impact of IT[2] on education. The research drew on thousands of primary sources and was highly selective in its inclusion of claims. Among the claims made one can see the breadth of IT's impact, for instance:

- IT can provide a safe and non-threatening environment for learning;

- IT has the flexibility to meet the individual needs and abilities of each student;
- IT gives students immediate access to a richer source of learning materials;
- IT offers the potential for effective group working.

In all of these examples the evidence is sustainable. IT does allow the facility for making mistakes; differentiation in alternative classroom strategies are supported; the CD-ROM and the Internet provide a rich resource for the inquisitive learner, and the technology allows learners to collaborate and share experiences. Further, if one concentrates on the personal computer, the claims made by *IT Works* are equally impressive.

- Computers help students to learn when used in well-designed meaningful tasks and activities.
- Computers can reduce the risk of failure at school.
- Computers give students the chance to achieve where they have previously failed.

The evidence on challenging and appropriate computer-based activities is extensive, showing where learners can benefit from a structured approach to investigative activities – for example, in visits to museums; older and mature students are not threatened by the pressures in classrooms; and that the simple word-processor facilitates expression and enables creative activities (CET, 1994). In all of these cases the evidence for a technology effect on education is compelling, but one does have to be careful of the evidence. Many claims need careful scrutiny. Although there are rigorous meta-analyses of effect sizes (Kulik *et al.*, 1980),[3] some of the evidence is anecdotal and descriptive in nature. In one of their seminal reviews, Kulik *et al.* write:

> 'in studies in which different teachers taught computer-based and conventional sections of a course, examination differences were more clear cut for computer-based teaching… where a single teacher taught both experimental and control classes, *differences were less pronounced.*'

Human intervention and the adaptability of individual teachers are significant variables in determining effect sizes. This warning is not damaging to the overall conclusion that IT or communications technology has had and continues to have a significant effect on the process and outcomes of teaching and learning. This 'technology *in* education' is an important driver for change and leaves a lasting effect, but is not the potential that was expected by the early programmed learning proponents referred to above. They saw a *systems approach* to education to be the main driver for change. In the 1960s the electronic digital computer could not have been seen in the way we see it now. Indeed, there are well-documented cases of major educational thinkers completely rejecting the influence of computers on their practice.[4] Technology in education has become a driver for change. What about the technology *of* education? What is this educational or instructional technology and what claims are made for its influence?

A TECHNOLOGY *OF* EDUCATION?

To understand this debate we need to define the various approaches to educational technology. David Mitchell, writing in the *Encyclopaedia of Educational Communications and Technology* (Unwin and McAleese, 1978), uses a definition by Gibson (1971) of educational technology as a masthead. He defines it as 'the systematic application of people, ideas, materials and equipment to the solution of educational problems... the process by which the learning materials are selected and produced and by which modes of communication are designed and arranged in the learning environment'. This cybernetic definition of educational technology is a much more prescriptive approach rather than a descriptive definition that concentrates on IT in education. In reality this technology of education has not had the significant influence in the UK and Europe that it has in the USA and Canada.

I will look at some of the theories[5] or components of instructional technology to show its influence and potential. Charlie Reigeleuth has written a number of books that describe, evaluate and provide examples of instructional theories (Reigeluth, 1987). He has drawn from sources as diverse as Lev Landa's Algo-heuristic Theory on the selection of content (Landa, 1974), through the many publications of Robert Gagné, Leslie Briggs and David Merrill (1978; 1977; 1983), which deal with sequencing and ordering of instructional elements. Reigeluth suggests a distinction between the *prescriptive* theory of instruction and the *descriptive* theories of learning. This is a helpful distinction as, in general, instruction theories are normative. They are based on empirical descriptive theories of learning but they are designed to highlight what educators *should be doing* as a result of what we know about cognition and the acquisition of ideas. I will not discuss further the work that has been undertaken in building a theory of learning. Readers should consult Entwistle (1988) for an extensive treatment. The important point to make is that the technology *of* education is based on theories of instruction – which themselves are supported by a developing framework of cognitive research – including learning theories. The tension I am discussing is between the instructional theories and the technology *in* education. I suspect that the same tension exists between the impact of IT (which draws from human factors research and computing science) and learning research, as between the educational technology and IT. Three instructional theories are sufficiently interesting, accessible and important to us to merit more detail. Elaboration theory (Reigeluth, 1987) is about the choices teachers need to make to ensure effective *sequencing* of ideas in learning activities. Motivation theory is about the importance of the *affective* dimension to learning outcomes. Cognitive flexibility theory is about the regulation of *personal meaning*.

ELABORATION THEORY

Elaboration theory is concerned with sequencing. Reigeluth (1987), writing on recent evidence that supports his Theory of Elaboration, provides a succinct summary of its elements. He takes an analogy of the zoom lens, suggesting that just as a zoom lens on a camera can allow a viewer to move from a wide angle view to a narrow focus, so the presentation of ideas should progress from the broad to the particular in instruction. He can draw on many other writers (Gagné, Bruner, Ausubel and Merrill) to support this claim. Reigeluth sees the problems of what to teach/learn first, second, third, etc as one of providing the right context or framework for the learner in an 'epitome'. The epitome is an instruction event that – for the learner – epitomizes or characterizes the nature of what is to be learned. An epitome as an instructional event does not summarize, rather it provides the cognitive scaffolding for knowledge acquisition.[6]

Reigeluth suggests in Elaboration theory that the designer[7] of learning events move from concrete to abstract, overview to detail. This approach is supported in learning theories (Entwistle, 1988). This theory of instruction allows the designer to use a sequence entailing the epitome, the elaboration, the summary, followed by the synthesis. Elaboration theory also allows for different types of sequencing. For example, conceptual elaboration can be distinguished from procedural elaboration. In this way educational technologists (designers) can build learning environments that support learners being able to know what (conceptual) as well as to know how (procedural).

Reigeluth has taken a major problem for both teacher and students ('what order can things be learned?') and provided a rigorous framework to allow designers to implement the sequencing of content. This is a major characteristic of an instructional theory and it is a characteristic of a technology *of* education. Such a technology should provide *prescriptive* advice to educational technologists. An instructional theory does not only describe how to change teaching and learning – it suggests that teaching and learning *should be changed* and as a consequence suggests how such changes should occur. In this way a technology of education suggests that sequencing of content is important. If the designer wishes to implement a system-driven sequencing strategy, a likely way of proceeding is provided.

MOTIVATION

The affective domain of educational processes and outcomes is often avoided. I believe this is for two reasons. First, affective outcomes are very difficult to measure and to observe. Second, there is a reluctance to get too close to the motives and feelings of learners. It is felt that learners are invaded when designers begin to provide opportunities for feelings to be expressed or recognized. This is a mistaken belief. Learning and coming to know are not achieved without intent or at least a passive willingness that learning can occur. I am excluding incidental learning that occurs on a daily basis, such as knowing who was travelling in what car in front of one when going to work. Instructional theories based on principles of learning are concerned with the social and intentional aspects of knowledge acquisition. As I suggested, there is a general avoidance of theories in instructional technology that help the designer make use of motivation. The exception is John Keller (1984) who has contributed several seminal papers and chapters in books. Keller has been seen to supplement other instructional theories and to 'open the door to making teaching and learning fun'. There is strong cognitive evidence that effort in learning activities affects performance. In general, the more effort an individual expends, the more performance is enhanced. Further, it can be shown that confidence felt by an individual improves effort. Traditional instructional design theories (eg, Gagné, Merrill) concentrate on *performance;* motivational theories concentrate on *effort.* Keller and others have asked what influences effort? Keller's ARCS model and McAleese and Gunn's ROSIE framework contribute to a technology of education by suggesting how designers should influence learning events and opportunities and so effect the effort learners expend on instructional events. Keller (1984) addressed the issue of the strategies that designers need to adopt to increase perceptual arousal (eg, novel or surprising events); or how inquiry arousal can be enhanced (eg, the use of rhetorical questions); or how variability in instructional events can maintain learner interest. McAleese and Gunn (1994) have suggested that there are five drivers that effect learner effort, as follows.

- *Relevance* – activities that connect learning to needs and motives.
- *Outcomes* – instructional events that indicate outcomes of activities.
- *Satisfaction* – strategies that manage extrinsic and intrinsic learner satisfaction.
- *Interest* – providing the events that sustain curiosity and attention.
- *Expectancy* – instructional events that are designed to develop learner confidence.[8]

As an example of the way a technology of education can draw on motivation theory, I will suggest ways in which confidence might be enhanced in learners. If, as suggested above, confidence affects effort and effort influences outcomes, then any strategies that give learners a sense of confidence should be used. An educational technologist can develop confidence in learners by using tests of performance, feedback, praise, advisement and knowledge of results. Here the focus is not on the order of events or the sequencing of ideas, rather on how the learner can make the most of time on task.

A motivational theory, if it is to be effective, will allow the educational technologist to influence the way the learner is given confidence as a result of activities. As we know, for example, that knowledge of results influences attention and performance, the designer can ensure that appropriate tests of performance are used to provide knowledge of results. The prescriptive nature of a technology of education will suggest instructional implication. Not only should designers be aware of knowledge of results, but they should *do* something to influence it. A technology of education influences the way learners approach learning and how their interaction with events is managed.

CONSTRUCTIVISM

I do not want to dwell on the enormous output on constructivism that has appeared over the last eight years. Rather I will take one cognitive theory of instruction – Rand Spiro's Cognitive Flexibility Theory (Spiro, 1988) – as an example of the way both the technology *of* education and the technology *in* education have been influenced by cognitive psychologists. Rand Spiro's work is largely concerned with what he calls 'ill structured domains of knowledge' (such as medical science, literary criticism), which are central to our higher education system. Spiro claims and provides supporting evidence for the observation that learners must apply knowledge flexibly *across diverse contents*. A graduate must know how and when to apply contextually acquired ideas in new and novel situations. For example, engineers must be able to take understandings of construction, derived in controlled contexts, and apply them to real-worlds constrained by their employer's work ethos.

Using schema assembly (from cognitive science), Spiro prescribes multiple representations of ideas and thus avoids over-simplification. Complexity and irregularity are accepted as part of the real world and learners are encouraged to see ideas from different contextual perspectives. Cognitive flexibility theory is also capable of contributing to the technology in education. Hypertext is an organizational framework that allows learners to associate or link ideas. The associations can be hard wired or user driven, using a model of the domain. Hypertext has been one of the technologies that computers have supported for at least ten years. Personal computers using hypertextual software[9] allow learners to navigate knowledge domains and so encounter the complexity of ideas in different context. Similarly, Web-based interfaces to resources on the Internet allow learners to encounter real-world complexity. Learners can find data, examples and procedures of real-world applications of academic ideas. Cognitive flexibility theory supports such browsing. Spiro calls this approach 'traversing the terrain of knowledge'. Again this instructional theory can influence what is learned and how it is learned.

Instructional theories provide the intellectual framework for the educational technologist. Such theories – the components of a technology of education – should have a deep influence on the practices of education and on the way teachers and learners operate. There is a battleground in education between the technology in education and the technology of education. As I suggested above, the dominant UK experience over the last 30 years has been the technology that derives from the artefacts of education. It may be that the technology *of* education is still too eclectic and itself ill-structured.

In the most recent Association for Educational and Communications Technology (AECT) definition of instructional technology, Seels (1995) suggests the following definition: 'Instructional Technology is the theory and practice of design, development utilization, management and evaluation of the processes and resources for learning'. This definition draws on technologies in education: eg, print technologies contribute to the development of instructional events; instructional theories which contribute to the design of instructional events; and theories of innovation and implementation which contribute to the utilization of instruction. The AECT definition is almost a catch-all for curriculum development. Indeed 'curriculum development' writings in the 1970s by Lawrence Stenhouse (1975) and others, look fresh and familiar when one operationalizes the AECT definition.

IMPLICATIONS

So far I have drawn a distinction between the way a technology of education has been dominant in the UK and the potential for a technology of education to play an important role. The tension may be healthy or it may stifle adoption and development. Healthy tensions occur less frequently. I believe we need to address the tension that exists. Leslie Cummings (1995) writing in the Association for the Advancement of Computing in Education journal, *Educational Technology Review,* about faculty resistance to educational technology, lists six barriers that disable the adoption of educational technology by faculty in American colleges. Although some of these barriers are familiar (eg, lack of resources, technology problems), he emphasizes the conceptual dissonance between traditional practices and the technology of education and the technology in education. This conceptual dissonance is at the heart of the tension I referred to above. Without being able to see when and if this tension is resolved, I can still suggest a number of implications for teachers and students. I will list the implications as a set of assertions. The assertions are:

- We need appropriate macro and micro structures to support teachers and learners;
- We need a normative learning technology in addition to instructional normative design theories;
- We need accreditation and recording of performance by both teachers and students.

Structures

We need institutional and national structures to:

- *support, link, develop, coordinate* and *disseminate*

educational technology. At the macro level, national organizations such as the Staff and Educational Development Association (SEDA) and the Association for Learning Technology (ALT) need to link practitioners. The educational technologist needs linkages with others – others who share the same assumptions and others who have different experiences. Without this support, individuals can become isolated and lack motivation and drive. Practitioners need appropriate meetings (conferences, workshops, seminars, colloquia) to enable them to communicate their expertise and to hear of new developments and evidence that supports intuitive approaches.

At the macro level there is a significant role for bodies such as the National Council for Educational Technology (NCET) to act as a marketplace. NCET needs to focus the interests of different stakeholders. Government, local authorities, industry, educational practitioners and research and development groups need to have a focus where their complementary ideas can be seen in concert. Although NCET does act as a focus, I believe it is too close to the technology *in* education perspective. NCET needs to represent not only what is possible through IT, but mediate the instructional technology evidence for practitioners and institutions.

At the micro level, we need to see the rebirth of the learning and education development units. Such units have existed for 20 years. In the early days they were either technology centres or staff development units. In the 1980s, they took on a more educational role but have lost their focus over the last few years. They have lost focus by being drawn between supporting technology developments – such as computer-based learning – and acting as institutional development units responsible for accreditation and appraisal. A similar lack of focus has been evident outside the UK, especially in Australia.

Even major Institutes for Educational Technology, such as the IET at the Open University in the UK, have less influence on the development of courses than they did 20 years ago. We need to have macro and micro structures that support practitioners, link disciplines, develop new theories and approaches, coordinate activities and disseminate best practice and well-founded research. With this in place, we have one element in the resolution of the tension between the IT view and the systems view.

LEARNING TECHNOLOGY

So far I have given little attention to the needs of learners. The discussion has been focused on the designer or the technology. It is clear that the partnership between the learner and the teacher needs to be emphasized. Without the active support of the learner, developments in IT and instructional technology are wasted. In fact I believe that we need to seek out a learning technology that encompasses the design of learning with the skills needed to make the most of it. In a number of publications (eg, McAleese *et al.*, 1994; 1995), I have written of the way study skills need to be developed. Students need skills to make the most of the opportunities developed with or without IT or computers. It is no good implementing a course based on elaboration theory without the learner having the appropriate skills to seek information, synthesize ideas, solve problems and communicate their intentions. We need to develop a raft of learning technology skills that range from making the most of the technology in education (eg, using IT to find appropriate resources over computer networks) to self-awareness skills that allow learners to reflect on and in action. The learner in control of their own learning environment is a powerful ally in developing effective courses.

RECOGNITION AND ACCREDITATION

The tension between the technology of education and the technology in education exists in part because there is often no way of recording or recognizing innovative practices or skills acquired. Accreditation of learning technology as a professional activity is overdue. If we can accredit teaching in higher education,[10] then we need to accredit those who practise as educational technologists. This accreditation will bring more professional competence to the individuals and development assessment criteria and practices. Institutions will have to recognize the development of teaching as an activity of equal importance to scholarship and research competence for promotion and special awards.

Of course, without outlet for scholarly work in journals, conferences and books and the recognition of the outputs, practitioners will not be willing to invest the time in developing a technology of education. Also learners who acquire skills other than the recognized skills of disciplines (engineering, medicine, law etc) need a way of recording such achievements. A national scheme exists in schools for recording a profile of achievements in addition to subject competence. This scheme needs to be extended to students in post- compulsory education. Employers want students to acquire transferable skills in addition to their degrees. Learners who have acquired a raft of learning technology skills will be well placed to make the most of this if such activities are recognized and recorded by institutions.

It is no good complaining about the lack of success of educational technology without addressing the fundamental issues. I believe that a technology of education has a real place in higher education when the structures are in place, when the enabling skills are in place and when we recognize the acquisition and performance of these skills as equally important to subject competence. If we are to see the initial promise realized, we need to reconsider our approach to both technologies.

NOTES

1. The terms 'technology of education', 'educational technology' and 'instructional technology' are used as synonyms in this chapter. There are, of course, subtle differences, but it is convenient here to make no distinction.

2. 'IT' is an uncomfortable term. In reality the term should be 'communications technology'. The information aspect (what is communicated) is often left out. In the information science view, IT includes 'information', ie content. In the general public sense, IT excludes 'information'and means communications technology.

3. Effect size is a metric developed to measure across study effects in terms of standard deviations. It is now commonly used to make meta-analysis studies.

4. One good example of the 'myopia' took place in 1959. John Nisbet (Professor of Education in Aberdeen University 1963–88 and major innovator in teaching and learning in the UK for some 40 years) was asked to respond to a series of questions put by an academic colleague on the likely impact of 'digital electronic computers' on the practices of the Education Department. The questions ranged from 'Would your department have regular heavy work for it?' to 'Is the obtaining of a digital computer of sufficient interest to… your staff to attend a meeting?'. In every case Nisbet replied 'No'. Yet within ten years the Education Department in Aberdeen University was a leading centre for quantitative research and has to this day pioneered the use of IT. Some six years after this rejection of computers, Professor Nisbet was a member of

the Association for Programmed Learning (in the UK). Indeed, he had made the first link with researchers interested in automated teaching in 1959. He had one of the few UK subscriptions to *Automated Teaching Bulletin*, published by the Rheem Califone Corporation. In fact, the origins of educational technology in the UK came from the very same departments in Aberdeen (Education and Psychology). Leaders of educational change in the 1960s could not and did not foresee the impact of technology *in* education. They did expect a significant impact from a technology *of* education.

5. The term 'theory' is over used or abused by writers in this field. Reigeluth (1987) describes 'theories of instruction'. We also read of 'theories of learning'. One would have to meet more rigorous criteria for a theory to be sustained. I would prefer 'framework' – with a framework, there is the logical possibility of adding elements and seeing how it might support evidence, data etc.

6. Ausubel uses the term 'advance organiser'. There is a similarity between Reigeluth's 'epitome' and Ausubel's 'advance organiser'. In both cases the instructional strategy provides a pre-instructional precept that effects the way the learners responds to subsequent ideas.

7. The term 'designer' is used here to mean anyone who constructs learning activities for learners. In general this is the teacher, but is common practice in computer-based learning developments for the designer to be someone with design skills working alongside the subject specialist.

8. McAleese and Gunn have based their framework on Keller's ARCS model – Attention, Relevance, Confidence and Satisfaction. John Keller made the initial framework that I have added to and I am indebted to him for his pioneering work.

9. There are many examples, probably the best known are HyperCard (for the Macintosh) and Guide (for the PC). Many current authoring languages for PCs allow hypertext links to be created between 'nodes' or ideas.

10. Recently different groups have become involved in the professional accreditation of teachers and staff developers in higher education. SEDA is providing a framework and an accreditation agency for this purpose. The accreditation of teachers in higher education is still voluntary but it is likely to become compulsory within a few years.

REFERENCES

Briggs, L (1977) *Instructional Design: Principles and Applications,* Educational Technology Publications, Englweood Cliffs, NJ.

Council for Educational Technology (CET)(1994) *IT Works,* CET, Coventry.

Cummings, L E (1995) 'Educational Technology: A Faculty Resistance View' (Part 1) and 'Challenges of Resources, Technology and Tradition' (Part 2), *Educational Technology Review,* Winter, 5, 18–20.

Entwistle, N (1988) *Styles of Learning and Teaching: An Integrated Outline of Educational Psychology,* David Fulton Publishers, London.

Gagné, R M (1978) *Conditions of Learning,* Holt, Rhinehart & Winston, New York.

Gibson, C D (1971) 'Future Directions in Educational Technology Design', *Instructional Technology and the Planning of School Plants* (Conference Report), Los Angeles, 26 February.

Gunn, C (1996) 'A Framework for Situated Evaluation of Learning Environments', PhD, Heriot-Watt University, Edinburgh.

Keller, J M (1984) 'Motivational Design', in *Encyclopedia of Educational Media Communications and Technology*, D Unwin and R McAleese (eds), Greenwood, Westport.

Kulik, J A, Kulik, C C and Cohen, P A (1980) 'Effectiveness of Computer Based College Teaching: A Meta Analysis of Findings', *Review of Educational Research*, **50**, 4, 525–44.

Landa, L (1974) *Algorithimisation in Learning and Instruction*, Educational Technology Publications, Englewood Cliffs, NJ.

McAleese, R (1978) 'The Nature and Dissemination of Educational Technology Knowledge: Lessons and Implications', *Scienta Pedagogica Experimentalis*, **17**, 1, 44–60.

McAleese, R and Gunn, C (1994) 'The Evaluation of Motivation in Learning – About Time', Heriot-Watt University, CLIVE Project, TLTP (also in Gunn, 1996, Appendix).

McAleese, R and Gunn, C (1995) *Support for Learning, Computer Assisted and Open Access Education*, Vol. 29, Kogan Page, London.

McAleese, R, Gunn, C and Granum, G (1994) *Designing for Learning: Computer Based Support for Study Skills*, Designing for Learning Vol. 28, Kogan Page, London.

Merrill, D (1983) 'Component Display Theory', in *Instructional Design Theories and Models: An Overview of the Current Status*, C Reigeluth (ed.), Lawrence Erlbaum, Hillside, NJ.

Mitchell, D (1978) 'Educational Technology', in *Encyclopedia of Educational Media Communications and Technology*, D Unwin and R McAleese (eds), Macmillan, London.

Programmed Learning (1964) Message from the Minister of Education, Sir Edward Boyle and Editorial, **1**, 1, 2–4.

Reigeluth, C (1987) *Instructional Theories in Action: Lessons Illustrating Selected Theories and Models*, Lawrence Erlbaum, Hillside, NJ.

Seeley Brown, J and Duiguid, P (1996) 'Situated Cognition and the Culture of Learning', *Educational Researcher*, **18**, 1, 32–42.

Seels, B and Richey, R (1995) *Instructional Technology: The Definition and Domains of the Field*, Association for Educational Communications and Technology, Washington DC.

Spiro, R (1988) *Cognitive Flexibility Theory: Advanced Knowledge Acquisition in Ill-structured Domains*, Technical Report 441, Reading Research and Education Centre, Centre for the Study of Reading, University of Illinois at Urbana-Champaign; also, Proceedings of Tenth Annual Conference on the Cognitive Science Society, Lawrence Erlbaum, Hillside, NJ.

Stenhouse, L (1974) *An Introduction to Curriculum Research and Development*, Heinemann, London.

SECTION II
Developing Strategies and Policies for Changing Universities

Chapter 6

Developing Strategies and Policies for Changing Universities

Dary Erwin

US CONTEXT OF THE CHANGING UNIVERSITY

Higher education in our Western culture is undergoing considerable change and scrutiny, and educators are struggling in their understanding and response. The rhetoric is becoming more severe from educational critics such as Perelman, who writes:

> Contrary to what the reformers have been claiming, the central failure of our education system is not inadequacy but excess... the principal barrier to economic progress today is a mind-set that seeks to perfect education when it needs only to be abandoned.' (Perelman, 1992, p.24)

Often the voices of these critics are faintly heard as a passing fad, but the facts do not support our silent response. This chapter explores the US context of the changing university. Between 1990 and 1993, US public spending on higher education in the average dropped by $7.76 billion (Report of the States, 1994). In trying to recoup the loss, public universities increased tuition costs at least 10% a year during this same period. In consequence, the public outcry was great (Lemann, 1996), and tuition caps were set in many states, thus eliminating or restricting a chief revenue source. US college costs were increasing at rates greater than even healthcare and faster than the Consumer Price Index (Baumol and Blackman, 1995).

The message for change should not be understood as limited to public and less renowned schools (Lemann, 1996). Budget shortfalls reach to the most reputable US institutions such as Harvard, Stanford, and Pennsylvania (Ehrenfeld, 1996). Consider the advice of the former secretary of Yale University:

'In education, the real outcome should be defined in educational terms, not in terms of money or jobs. But the message is clear. Institutions of higher learning are going to have to do a far better job of explaining what they are asking people to pay for, and what the value of it is.' (Chauncey, 1995, p.30)

Kean, former president of Drew University, is more blunt:

'People are questioning our mission and questioning who we are. They claim we cost too much, spend carelessly, teach poorly, plan myopically, and when we are questioned, we act defensively.' (*Stress on Research*, 1994)

Acting either defensively or inadequately threatens greater loss of governance, autonomy, and security.

To the individual staff member, these financial shortfalls leading to less travel money, larger class sizes (Sutherland, 1995), and frozen vacant positions might be mistakenly perceived as a temporary down turn in the economic cycle (*The Economist*, 1994). In my own state of Virginia, the Secretary of Education withheld salary increases until universities established a serious post-tenure review system. Similar events will continue to affect the working lives of individual staff until we react and respond actively.

When help was solicited from the business community, business leaders were unsympathetic, demanding that higher education restructure itself before support would be forthcoming. For example, the Business–Higher Education Forum to the Education Commission of the (US) states, 'our stakeholders bemoan the widening gap between the priorities for which they *send* resources and the objectives for which higher education institutions *spend* it' (Munitz, 1995, p.10). Of course, business organizations have been undergoing significant change and revitalization (Ehrenfeld, 1996), and business wonders why educators do not listen more to their needs. The sizeable growth of business training centres such as Motorola University and McDonald Hamburger U should serve to awaken us. Fortunately, most of these companies who operate schools wish to offer training and not education. However, some public preference is emerging, for instance, for a certificate in Novell networking instead of completion of a Master of Business Administration degree.

Although the college degree is valued more than ever, the content of what is learned is under question. Munitz (1995) reports public worries about decreased attention to undergraduate teaching, overemphasis on graduate education, anarchic curricula, and ill-defined or absent measures of quality (Munitz, 1995, p.10). He goes on to pose the ubiquitous question: 'what are we paying for?'

In general, educators must act to define better their purposes with students, evaluate better student learning, and use this information to improve our instructional approaches. These steps are more than a process but an actual shift in paradigms from a teaching emphasis to learning emphasis.

TEACHING TO LEARNING

'And gladly wolde he lerne, and gladly teche' (*The Canterbury Tales, Prologue*)

Referring to this quote from Chaucer written in the 14th century, O'Banion (1996) has asserted that higher education has focused more on the teaching part than the learning part. Educators have thought that if they paid attention to the way they presented education, it was assumed that learning would occur; but learning does not necessarily happen.

In the future, the ways in which students learn will vary greatly. US universities in particular will be forced to break out of the 'time and place bound architecture of education' (O'Banion, 1996, p.1). There will be shifts from semester credit hours possibly to demonstration of competencies learned, and from designated class minutes in lecture to self-paced learning time spent in a variety of settings and modules. US educators have much to learn from their UK counterparts who have long emphasized less structured learning approaches, yet technology will infuse change in the UK system too. Instead of varying the ways to certify learning and keeping instructional approaches fairly set and structured, the future will find varying instructional approaches and more constant methods of certification. Learning options or instructional approaches might include portable modules developed by national professional associations or corporations, stand-alone technological systems such as IBM's *Ulysses* and Philips Interactive Media *The World of Impressionism*, tutor-led groups, project-based activities, and service learning (O'Banion, 1996, p.4).

Consider the proposal by US governors to establish a 'virtual university' in the expansive western part of the US. Recognizing the high labour costs of teaching and the reluctance to build new physical campuses, technology is viewed by these budget-setters as the viable alternative. Although the effectiveness of technology is not established as a *replacement* to instruction, the seriousness of their ideas cannot be ignored. The Open University in the UK is certainly a strong model for the US to study.

Whether countries have 'virtual universities' is not the only point of change in this example, however. The absence of credible and valid systems of programme evaluation and assessment about learning remains a surprise to persons outside higher education. The strongest advocate of the virtual university, Colorado Governor Roy Romer, states, 'But the certification of what is learned has always been in the hands of the university. We're coming into the age where that is going to be blown apart' (Blumenstyk, 1995, p.A20). Our role in the assessment process is under question, and educators must work hard to remain central in the certification process.

THE ROLE AND PROCESS OF ASSESSMENT

Whatever the national system of higher education, the credibility of our institutional marking and evaluation processes is at an all-time low. At least four countries, Britain, Denmark, France and The Netherlands, have established some type of quality assurance programme (Desruisseaux, 1994). Although these systems differ, Westerheijden and van Vught (1995) identify four common characteristics of the European quality assessment systems:

1. A separate coordinating agency overseeing the assessment process.
2. A strong role for self-evaluation and external reviews.
3. Public communication of results.
4. Use of results in decision-making processes from teaching to administrative staff levels.

In the US, the accreditation system is under threat of demise because of the lack of credible information in the accreditation review process. In the past, an over-reliance was evident on using the amount of resources, such as library books, or percentage of teaching staff with doctorates as measures of educational quality. Lately, the peer review process is under question, with doubt over the objectivity and worth of the observations. Opinions are having less priority over hard data about quality.

In spite of the advent of these centralized systems, there is still a strong reliance on the information produced by individual campuses. Occasionally for financial reasons, and at other times for credibility reasons, institutions are developing more extensive systems of programme evaluation and assessment in Europe (Desruisseaux, 1994) and in the US (Erwin, 1991). For institutions wishing to establish or review their programme assessment and evaluation processes, several steps will be mentioned here.

First, clear statements about *what is to be learned* are necessary. One cannot know how to assess something without identifying what it is. Again the practice has been more commonplace in the UK than the US to have programme objectives (or learning outcomes). Objectives about knowledge, skills such as technology, or developmental characteristics should provide clear direction for teaching, for programme assessment, and for the public who wish to understand more about education. This understanding is even more important for non-traditional college entrants.

Educators are typically familiar with knowledge and skills but are more uncertain about the last category of developmental characteristics. Consider the construct of flexibility and openness toward different thoughts and people. An institution might assess students' degree of flexibility and openness to study, for example, the effects of study abroad programmes where students are exposed to different cultures and ideas. Developmental characteristics are often difficult to describe, yet they are some of the longer-lasting aspects of the collegiate experience, especially given the fast changing nature of knowledge.

Second, *choose or design assessment methods that are based on the programme objectives.* Occasionally, assessment methods exist through proprietary testing organizations or from professional groups, and teaching staff must systematically judge the fit between institutional programme objectives and an existing assessment method. More than likely, teaching staff will design their own assessment method. A later section of this chapter, 'Methods of Assessment', describes a process for designing one type of assessment methods. Additional examples of programme objectives and types of assessment method may be found in Erwin (1991).

A third step in the assessment process involves strategies for collecting assessment information. The advent of modules in the UK and semester-based systems in the US provide opportunities for collecting and using assessment information for diagnostic feedback. Unfortunately, some institutions focus entirely on the end-point for programme feedback when it is too late to instil any 'mid-course corrections'. Collecting assessment information associated with module or particular instructional approach gives staff feedback about that unit.

End-of-programme assessments are still needed, but study of the various components helps to identify strengths and weaknesses in a diagnostic way. Using only end-point assessment information limits generalizations about progress made during the curriculum interventions. More institutions are moving to collecting assessment information at matriculation, then following up retesting at mid-undergraduate point, then collecting assessment information towards the end of the programme. Points of progress allow institutions to allow for varying entry levels of students and for examining change over time (see Feldt and Brennan, 1989, for methodological issues regarding change scores).

Fourth, several strategies for analysing assessment information should also be considered in the planning and implementation of an institutional assessment programme. Change over time has already been mentioned as one strategy. Multiple assessment collection points studied in conjunction with modules and semesters also are valuable. It is not enough to measure learning itself; there are always questions about why some students learn more than other students. Is the structure of the module or semester related to student learning? How long should a module be? Is the module integrated in a sequence? To what extent does technology improve student learning? To what extent to student characteristics relate to the module content instructional approach? What out-of-class experiences best reinforce in-class teaching?

Consider our assessment study (Erwin and Rieppi, 1995) about the impact of a multimedia classroom for teaching a variety of undergraduate psychology courses or modules. Students were divided into multimedia or traditional lecture sections and compared on common examinations at the end. In addition, students' tendency as visual learning discriminators, auditory oriented, or haptic-oriented learners were assessed in relation to learning of knowledge in abnormal, statistics, and physiological psychology courses. Differences in student learning due to technology and to type of preferred learning were studied. Assessment studies especially about various technology models and other types of instructional modules will become more typical in the future. As mentioned earlier, the extent to which technologically delivered instruction can replace human interactions is a basic question.

Much attention was given in the first part of this chapter to the use of information by external examiners. The individual teaching staff at institutions will always have a strong role to play in generating assessment information because of the complexities involved. Institutional educators are in the optimum positions to study the value of various instructional approaches. It is our option as educators whether to participate fully or have other persons evaluate us.

The quality and nature of assessment methods needs additional planning and design by teaching staff and evaluators. For instance, grades and marks are under attack for 'grade inflation' or too many high marks. The next section briefly addresses this topic of assessment methods with some suggestions for the design of rating scales and checklists.

METHODS OF ASSESSMENT

Essentially, these are two primary ways for evaluating students' abilities: the selective response format and the constructed response format. The selective response format presents a content test item followed by available choice from which the student selects the best available answer. Multiple-choice or true/false questions are the two most popular selective response formats. This paper will illustrate the other type, the constructed response format, but design tips pertaining to selective response formats are available elsewhere (eg, Erwin, 1991; Isaacs, 1994).

A constructed response format elicits an active learning performance, product, process, or personal trait from students for assessment review. Examples of these stimuli include for performance, an artistic production; for a product, an essay, article, or computer programme; for a process, a scientific laboratory exercise or therapy session; and for a personal trait, academic/learning autonomy or ethical approach. Overlap, of course, exists across these categories.

The student constructions of performance, product, process, or personal traits are typically evaluated in the US with a rating scale or checklist. A rating scale consists of a series of statements or items that describe various qualitative levels of behaviour (Erwin, 1991). Such a scale contains a variety of components or aspects important for the successful completion of the construction. For example, one may define writing ability to be composed of word usage, sentence construction, organization, content, mechanics, support and focus. Each component is rated on a continuum from 'poor' to 'excellent'. The most effective rating scale contains behavioural anchors or descriptors for this continuum, rather than vague terms such as 'poor' or 'good'. Numerical continuums such as one to five without behavioural anchors are also too vague for common understanding and are therefore unreliable. A sample scenario with a group process component from an interpersonal communication rating scale is given next.

After observing students in a small group setting during a problem solving situation, each group member is rated. 'When group members offer opinions, how does the student respond?'

(a) Actively seeks others' opinions. Listens closely, integrates and synthesizes any new information that can be used.

(b) Dependent on others opinions to help make final decisions. Has trouble making independent decisions without approval of the group.

(c) Ignores opinions of others when offered. Argues if members disagree with own point of view. Refuses to consider other opinions as helpful.

(d) Listens to opinions given by other group members but unable to integrate those opinions to strengthen own arguments and information. Becomes hostile if own opinions not taken.

After viewing students' interacting, each student is rated in one of the above four categories.

A checklist is a close alternative to a rating scale if there is no continuum or qualitative levels of behaviour. Checklists just list a series of behaviours or characteristics that the student either exhibits or does not exhibit. For example, when evaluating a public speech, such a checklist might include these attributes: major ideas properly established and identified, and adapted message to the audience. Trained staff or evaluators would then check each attribute for its presence or absence. Deciding on the components of a successful or unsuccessful performance, product, process, or trait is the key to the rating sheet or checklist.

Smode *et al.* (1962, p.46) outlined seven aspects of performance measures that can be reflected in the components of rating scale:

1. **Time**: for example, how long does it take a hygiene student to fluorinate teeth?

2. **Accuracy**: for example, to what degree is the student's solution correct for a given problem?

3. **Frequency of occurrence**: for example, how often does the student social worker exhibit distracting behaviours while in therapy with a client?

4. **Amount achieved or accomplished**: for example, how much money has a student 'earned' in a simulated business portfolio of investments?

5. **Consumption or quantity used**: for example, how much of a chemical compound remains in a solution in a general chemical experiment?

6. **Behaviour**: for example, when members of a group are presented with a problem to solve, such as in a case study, how able is each member to (a) define the problem; (b) suggest alternatives; and (c) help resolve conflicts?

7. **Condition or state of the individual in relation to the task**: for example, when presented with multicultural diversity, how tolerant is the student?

Aspects 1–5 elicit frequency counts or amounts. Aspects 6 and 7 are more common categories for rating scales and call for more subjective judgements (Erwin 1991, pp.85–6).

The relevance of the performance, product, process, or trait is crucial; the student exhibition of the actual work desired is very educational. For instance, more institutions are assessing the accumulation of student work in portfolios. Educators or tutors using portfolios should address these three areas before initiating the process. Firstly, what is the purpose of the portfolio and how will the data be used? Secondly, what will be in the portfolio? And thirdly, how will the portfolio be evaluated?

Responsibility for the content of the portfolio is typically the students; however, guidelines for the type of work in the portfolio comes from the educator or tutor. For example, if the student is required to assemble an artistic part of the portfolio, are the artistic products created by the students, or chosen by the student then evaluated? How many artistic products should be assembled? Some structure is necessary for the portfolio, otherwise assessors may not have the samples needed to make an evaluation.

Occasionally, the idea of design and collection of assessment information conjures the notion of an extra workload for teaching staff. This is true in the beginning with the construction of the rating scale or checklist. However, once the rating scales or checklists are established, the evaluation process goes rather quickly. In addition, comprehensive rating scales or checklists are usually welcomed by students because they provide clear expectations and clear feedback, and the review itself is educational in nature.

USING ASSESSMENT INFORMATION

This chapter has presented the need for assessment, an example for designing one type of assessment method, and now describes the most important aspect of the assessment process: use of assessment information. Some departments and institutions go through the motions of conducting assessment studies and never use the information, other than to satisfy external examiners. One criteria for evaluating assessment programmes is noting the various uses of assessment results. It is incumbent upon educators to demonstrate how programmes are being improved, based on empirical results.

Within the department, tutors and teaching staff may change the content of the curriculum and change the way it is delivered using assessment results as guidance. Creation and content within modules or courses, types of hiring decisions, emphasis on passages of module or course content, the nature of student assignments, the type of extra curricular or lecture supplemental activities are examples of changes guided by assessment results. As explained earlier, the establishment of modules provide a wonderful opportunity for more effectively structuring learning units and activities.

Within the institution, more decisions about resource allocations are being made based on results of quality. Requests for resources are usually followed by statements such as 'How do you know this new resource is needed?' Often, illustrating programme weaknesses provides more powerful evidence for resources than arguing without data. In the US with the peer review system under attack, harder databased evidence is gaining more credibility than professional opinion alone.

Within higher education systems, assessment information aggregated across institutions is useful in arguing for resources against other requests for public monies. Aggregated assessment information across certain types of institutions is also wanted by persons wishing to understand what education is doing in a broader sense. Understandably some complexity is lost; however, the gain is tremendous from government officials reluctant to allocate further monies without increased awareness of the mysterious outcomes of graduates.

Teaching staff have a central role in this process of shaping learning outcomes. In the US, government officials will substitute outputs such as graduation and retention rates for data about the outcomes of learning if these are unavailable. Educators have a responsibility to keep the focus on learning rather than outputs or other efficiency measures that represent our work only tangentially.

In summary, the process of assessment mirrors the academic process: state one's hypotheses about what is to be learned, collect information about those hypotheses, and confirm and revise those hypotheses based on results. Citizens look to educators to model this process not just to teach about this process in their disciplines. The assessment process is a responsibility in which many audiences are watching for our response. To fail to establish credible institutional assessment systems and to use this assessment information for programme improvement and public understanding is to invite further erosion of financial support for higher education and self governance for teachers.

REFERENCES

Baumol, W and Blackman, S (1995) 'How to Think About Rising College Costs', *Planning for Higher Education*, **23**, 4, 1–7, University of Michigan, Ann Arbor, Michigan.

Blumenstyk, G (1995) 'Campuses in Cyberspace: Western Governors Will Explore The Establishment of a Virtual University', *The Chronicle of Higher Education*, A18–21, Washington DC.

Breneman, D (1995) *Higher Education: On a Collision Course with New Realities*, AGB Occasional Paper No 22, Charlottesville, VA.

Chauncey, Jr, H (1995) 'A Calm Before the Storm?' *Yale Alumni Magazine*, **58**, 7, 30–31, New Haven, CT.

Desruisseaux, P (1994) 'Assessing Quality', *The Chronicle of Higher Education*, **7** December, A41–42, Washington DC.

Ehrenfeld, T (1996) 'What to Chop?' *Newsweek*, 29 April, 59–68, Washington DC.

Erwin, T D (1991) *Assessing Student Learning and Development*, Jossey-Bass, San Francisco, CA.

Erwin, T D and Rieppi, R (1995) 'A Comparison of Multimedia and Traditional Classrooms Teaching Undergraduate Psychology Courses', Paper presented at the Annual Conference on Teaching of Psychology, March, Ellenville, NY.

Feldt, L S and Brennan, R L (1989) in *Educational Measurement*, 3rd edn, R L Linn (ed.), Macmillan, New York.

Isaacs, G (1994) *Multiple Choice Testing: A Guide to the Writing of Multiple Choice Tests and to their Analysis*, Higher Education Research and Development Society of Australia, Campbelltown, Australia.

Knight, P (ed.)(1995) *Assessment for Learning in Higher Education*, Kogan Page, London.

Lemann, N (1996) 'With College for All', *Time,* 10 June, 67–8, Chicago, IL.

Munitz, B (1995) 'Wanted: New Leadership for Higher Education', *Planning for Higher Education,* **24**, 9–16, University of Michigan, Ann Arbor, MI.

O'Banion, T (1996) 'Gladly Would He Learn', *On the Horizon,* **4**, 3–5. Jossey-Bass San Francisco, CA.

Perelman, L J (1992) *School's Out: A Radical New Formula for the Revitalization of America's Educational System,* Avon Books, New York.

Report of the States (1994) *American Association of the State Colleges and Universities,* Washington DC.

Smode, A F, Gruber, A, and Ely, J H (1962) 'The Measurement of Advanced Flight Vehicle Crew Proficiency in Synthetic Ground Environments', Report MRL-TDR-62-2, Wright-Patterson Air Force Base, Aerospace Medical Division, Ohio.

Stress on Research and Education at Colleges and Universities: Institutional and Sponsoring Agency Responses (1994) Report of Collaborative Inquiry conducted jointly by the National Science Board and the Government–University–Industry Research Roundtable, July, Washington DC.

Sutherland, J (1995) 'Down and Out in the British University', *Lungua Franca,* 54–9, New York.

The Economist (1994) 'Towers of Babble', 25 December, 72–4, London.

Westerheijden, D F and van Vught, F A (1995) 'Assessment of Quality in Western Europe', *Assessment Update,* **7**, 2, 1–11, Jossey-Bass, San Francisco, CA.

Wingspread Group on Higher Education (1993) *An American Imperative: Higher Expectations for Higher Education,* Racine, WI.

Chapter 7

QILT: A Whole-Institution Approach to Quality Improvement in Learning and Teaching

Mike Laycock

INTRODUCTION

In recent years, the University of East London has been engaged in an evaluation of its quality assurance procedures, particularly those associated with the academic review of courses. A small working party examining Teaching and Learning Review was concerned not to replicate systems of the past and proposed a radical alternative, formally entitled Quality Improvement in Learning and Teaching (QILT). The focus on improvement or enhancement was a deliberate reconsideration of the model of review, seen as a deficit-focused or 'autopsy model' of quality assurance.

WHAT IS QILT?

Essentially, QILT is a process which involves the creation, by academic departments/subject groups, of funded improvement plans, their implementation, and the formative and summative evaluation of progress (Figure 7.1).

Working with an adviser (every faculty has at least one adviser who receives remission from teaching duties to fulfil their role), each department/ subject team undertakes a regular and iterative cycle of quality improvement. The team is relatively organic and dependent on the priorities identified. It has teaching staff and student involvement but may also include allied staff (from student services, the library etc).

The cycle has three phases. In phase one, staff construct an improvement plan which provides statements of areas where improvements are to be made, a timetable for achieving them, an appropriate staff development programme and finally, identifies appropriate evaluation criteria and evidence to measure outcomes. Funding is allocated to support the plan from the central staff development budget to each faculty to an equitable funding formula, to pay for QILT initiatives. Plans are approved by the faculty Educational Development Sub-Committees with advice from the QILT Adviser.

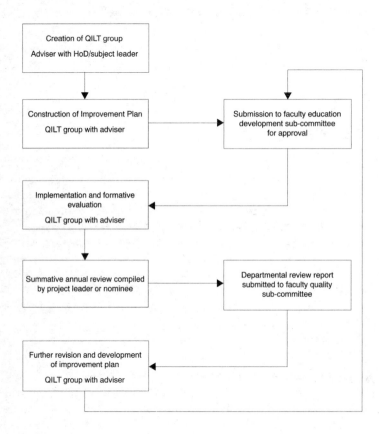

Figure 7.1 *The QILT process*

Phase two represents the process of implementation and formative evaluation where the activities might include staff development workshops, the production of materials, changes in teaching methods – whatever has been identified in the plan. Although this is UEL's internal process of quality enhancement the QILT Handbook identifies the new HEFCE Core Areas (Circular 39/94) as potential improvement areas.

Finally, in phase three, staff evaluate whether improvements have been achieved and are effective and take action as appropriate. The outcomes of QILT improvements will contribute to the internal annual departmental review (the QILT cycle is repeated annually), to internal, quinquennial Subject Reviews and to the HEFCE self-assessment exercise. QILT is the University's Enterprise in Higher Education continuation strategy and is centrally coordinated by the former Enterprise Director (now the QILT Co-ordinator) within UEL's Educational Development Services.

WHY WAS QILT INTRODUCED?

A number of issues informed UEL's shift of emphasis towards a complementary model of quality improvement. The first relates to the dubious value of quality assurance alone in providing a model to create change. One of the critical issues for the whole area of QA, with its emphasis on achieving accountability by emphasizing formalized methods and written procedures, is that it could be said to be valid for a stable, uncompetitive environment. Partly because of governmental pressure, that environment no longer exists. Higher education is currently coping with very volatile internal and external pressures, an accelerated pace of change and vigorous competition. The sector's ability to cope with change requires radical alternatives in the way it responds to it. Continuous examination and assessment of the methods and procedures of quality assurance alone will not provide the impetus for change. A shift towards an enhancement-led system may provide that impetus and permit institutions to anticipate change.

Yorke (1994) has argued for such an enhancement-led quality system and has proposed that Funding Councils should specifically earmark funding for the enhancement of teaching and learning. This could be set alongside the 'core funding in respect of student numbers and funding specifically targeted at research'. He proposes that each institution should have the opportunity to bid to the relevant funding council for what might be termed learning development (or 'DevL' funding). Such an approach, he argues, reduces the pressure on institutions to adopt a more defensive position with regard to the current assessment exercise adopted by the HEFCE.

QILT provides the basis upon which any funding regime could have public evidence of quality improvement in such a bidding process. The university has its own DevL funding system in microcosm and now has the potential for submitting such plans which, critically, are oriented to the six HEFCE core areas for self-assessment. Thus the university's QILT programme seeks to provide a contribution to the national debate about the relative merits of the approaches to quality adopted by the HEFCE and the HEQC. The recent pressure from vice-chancellors for the formation of a single agency may move further forward if universities can be seen to be transparently self-regulatory and self-regenerating both in the areas of assurance *and* enhancement.

Secondly, our traditional organizational structures may be becoming unsuitable for effective communication and may actually retard the process of change. The mistake made by institutions (and by government), is that educational change can be accomplished by trying to introduce system reforms, tighter forms of planning and management, reorganization, and so on. Although HEIs place great reliance on the democratic process enshrined in committee work and the institutional value of hierarchical management structures, the pace of change is beginning to render these organizational forms unwieldy. Both the structures, and the managerial activity emanating from them, may founder if all those who are involved in the institution do not have some stake in managing that change. It requires the empowerment of all staff to become involved in continuous improvement so that they are committed to, and own, the process of change.

THE TRANSFORMATIONAL POWER OF QILT

A learning organization?

Kolb's model of the experiential learning cycle informed the university's EHE programme both as a process for staff development/learning and as a model for student learning. That same model is now operating as an institutional framework for the QILT process (Figure 7.2). The model provides the basis for creating a learning organization at UEL. It should also be clear, in terms of the national debate, that quality enhancement and quality assurance need not be seen as mutually exclusive but rather as elements within a continuous, iterative quality improvement cycle. A single UK agency for assuring quality might usefully acknowledge the importance of these elements in attempting to generate both a dynamic and reflective HE system.

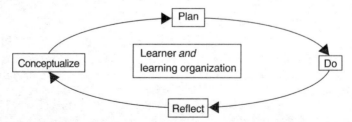

Figure 7.2 *Kolb's experiential learning cycle (adapted from Henry, 1989)*

A 'new collegiality'?

QILT also has transformational power in terms of providing a culture for the reconceptualization of the process of change management and accountability for it. Traditional processes, as Woodhouse (1994) has observed, are complex:

'Unlike a business with a clear management structure, in a university no individual has overriding power of action, but many have enough power for obstruction, and decision-making is difficult, even in the most minor matters. Change in a university comes about through many tiny increments, no one of which is large enough to rock the boat. These increments are represented as small reasonable remedies in response to great pressures, and take account of personal and territorial interests...[where]...everyone must agree, but no one is accountable.'

That pressure for accountability despite, or perhaps because of, a declining unit of resource, has introduced a new scepticism among academic staff, not only in terms of the difficulty of delivering quality in such circumstances, but also related to the concern about the rise of managerialism. Increased demands for academic freedom have been couched not in terms of 'freedom to' but more a 'freedom from' this perceived increase in managerialism. However, others have suggested that these pressures for accountability will mean systemic changes in the management of HE towards a more 'collegial culture':

'Universities will change considerably over the next decade, and one of the main forces for the change will be this pressure to make them accountable for students' learning... The main change will be towards the development of more collegial, corporate cultures, with individual academics being more closely associated with the departmental teaching teams, and with departments working towards similar goals... The goal is to achieve a simultaneous loose–tight coupling in HE organizations; tight on values and procedures, loose on ways in which those values and procedures are expressed and assessed.' (Knight, 1994)

UELs approach is designed to develop a collective ethos based on this 'loose–tight coupling'. QILT is tight on the promotion of processes and procedures but loose in the way that staff teams approach their definitions of quality improvement. The ethos is not derived from securing agreement at committee level about policy statements, nor by managerial dictate, but by ensuring maximum participation and involvement in change by the university as a collectivity. It demands an approach which relies on teamwork and a consensus, which, as Taylor and Hill (1994) have suggested is something that is problematic in HE:

'namely the provision of an appropriate and enriching learning experience for every student. For some establishments there may be a need to spend time reaching consensus on this point alone. This deceptively simple concept, once embraced, will effect the removal of barriers between departments, between academics and administrators arguing over points of territory or procedure and between academics entrenched in "functional foxholes" or "discipline dug-outs".'

Harvey (1995) suggests that there has been renewed interest in the concept of collegialism in the UK and that it 'can be characterized as having taken two paths – a conservative tendency and a radical alternative'. He describes the former as 'cloisterism' and the latter as the 'new collegialism'. Both have emerged as a consequence of the perceived growth in managerialism but are at opposite ends of the spectrum so far as reaction to that managerialism is concerned.

A range of concepts are used to codify the cultural and educational orientations of both. Academic cloisterism is described as 'inward-looking, individualistic, self-serving and self-regulating, characterized by esoteric knowledge and opacity'. The new collegialism, by contrast, is said to be:

'outward looking and responsive; emphasizes continuous improvement; professional accountability; encourages team-working; focuses on the total student experience; views students as participants in the process of learning rather than as a customer or as an end-product; and focuses on the outcomes of higher education as well as the process.'

Harvey equates the two cultures with particular orientations to teaching and learning. Thus a cloisterist 'sees students as novices to be initiated into the mysteries of the discipline' and the skills and abilities expected of students are 'often implicit and obscure'. New collegialism, by contrast, is 'learning-oriented. It focuses on facilitating student learning rather than teaching, and explicitly encourages the development of a range of skills and abilities. It prefers transparency to obscurity.'

Since the QILT approach itself demands a culture of participation, teamworking, networking, innovation, and the empowerment of staff, is the generation of that 'new collegial' culture sufficient to promote a transformation in approaches to teaching and learning?

A range of other factors, of course, have also provided the impetus for changes to teaching and learning methods, not the least of which have been the changing nature of student intake, both in number and diversity, changing modes of provision towards modularization and semesterization and UK-wide initiatives such as the Enterprise in Higher Education (EHE) initiative. But if QILT has a transformational power in terms of shifts in teaching and learning practices, these should at least be observable in the outcomes of the process. The university has now undergone the first phase of QILT. It is time to reflect on its potential.

QILT IMPROVEMENT PLANS 1994/5

There is clear evidence from the 55 QILT Improvement Plans presented for 1994/5 funding from all departments in the university, that staff at UEL are addressing the central problems and issues faced by this university, namely:

- a readiness to engage in the democratization of the management of change and the development of a new collegial culture;
- the need for increasing efficiency and effectiveness while continuing to provide a quality learning experience for students;
- the teaching and learning implications of modularization and semesterization;
- the increasing heterogeneity of the student body;
- the need to share good practice across the institution and beyond;
- the need for a heightened awareness of planning in the quality process;
- the need to address systematically the recommendations and requirements emanating from accreditation, course and external examiner reports, student feedback, etc;
- the importance of student involvement in the planning, implementation *and* evaluation process of quality improvement – the generation of a cooperative learning environment.

A wide range of areas for improvement have been identified by all departments/subject groups. Nevertheless, some areas have featured more prominently in this first round.

Improving student handbooks

The improvement of student handbooks should not be regarded as an activity simply consistent with the requirements of UEL's *Quality Manual.* Handbooks are becoming the focus for curriculum development and improved teaching and learning methods. For example, issues such as the clear identification of learning objectives/outcomes, the development of assessment methods consistent with those objectives, the articulation of assessment criteria, the inclusion of learning resources (selected readings, etc) and the inclusion of student feedback instruments have all become facets of development that demonstrate an attention to 'student-centred' learning. The noticeable power shift is in rendering explicit to students that which was formally implicit, thus enabling them to take more responsibility for their own learning.

The second important signal presented by this improvement is the apparent desire for consistency in practice. This is not an internally imposed culture, but, being identified by teaching staff, is both a means of coping with, and progressing modularization in the face of declining resources and an acknowledgement that an equitable treatment of students is essential.

Computer-based/enhanced learning

In those areas of the institution where staff skill levels are high, the opportunities presented by computer based/enhanced learning are being vigorously addressed. Some will highlight the dangers of a depersonalized learning experience. But with the advent of larger classes, opportunities for interaction become fewer in the traditional lecture. Carefully constructed, interactive multimedia packages may permit the release of time formally spent in more traditional teaching activities so that staff can devote the time gained to more seminar and tutorial work.

Assessment

There is some indication in QILT plans that staff are addressing the difficulties presented by modularization (and particularly semesterization) in the assessment process. This is leading to a re-examination of the *purpose* of assessment. The dangers are perceived as both structural ('assessment bottlenecks') and educational (an 'assessment-driven' system). Both are seen as reducing the possibilities for 'learning through assessment'. The message derived from these plans is that increasing resources are being devoted to an assessment system that is providing fewer opportunities for learning.

Skills development

Staff at UEL, and elsewhere, are more aware of the need for study skills support for an increasingly heterogeneous student body, and the need to develop and assess transferable skills. Employment trends away from 'stable vocations' to a more varied career pattern, indicate the need for the development of an HE culture which addresses personal and professional capability, lifelong learning and flexibility as well as an appropriate knowledge base and skills of critical analysis.

IN SUMMARY

As a model for self-improvement, QILT does not confine itself to those areas conventionally described as 'teaching and learning'. UEL's mission concentrates on improving the 'total student experience'. All who work and learn at the university contribute to the improvement of that experience and the overall learning and teaching environment. QILT for allied staff has already been piloted by the institution. Since it is intended as a whole-institution programme it is essential that there is no status divide. For the future, QILT may involve a range of teams of people, not necessarily confined to teaching departments, and provide a dynamic foil for the university's current structures.

Clearly, the QILT process at UEL is in its infancy and sweeping claims for its effectiveness in terms of its objectives would be premature. Its potential as a model for teamworking, its capacity for involving those staff and students who have a stake in solving particular problems, will be the key to its success. Perhaps, more importantly, the university has public evidence, from a model which is transferable to any HE institution, of a credible means of both self-assurance and self-improvement.

REFERENCES

Harvey, L (1995) *Quality Assurance Systems, TQM and the New Collegialism*, QHE, University of Birmingham, Birmingham.

Higher Education Funding Council for England (HEFCE)(1994) *The Quality Assessment Method from April 1995*, Circular 39/94, HEFCE.

Henry, J (1989) 'Meaning and Practice in Experiential Learning', in *Making Sense of Experiential Learning: Diversity in Theory and Practice*, S Warner Weil and I McGill (eds), SRHE/Open University, Milton Keynes

Knight, P (1994) 'Turmoil in Success: The Assessment of Teaching Quality', in *Quality Assurance in Education*, Vol 1 No 1, MCB University Press Ltd.

Taylor, A and Hill, F (1994) 'Quality Management in Education', *Quality Assurance in Education*, Vol 1, No 1, MCB University Press Ltd.

Woodhouse, D (1994) 'TQM in HE: A Sceptical View', in *Quality Assurance in Education and Training: Conference Papers*, Vol 2, pp.25–8, New Zealand Qualifications Authority (NZQA), Wellington.

Yorke, M (1994) 'Enhancement-Led Higher Education', in *Quality Assurance in Education*, Vol 2, No 3, MCB University Press Ltd.

The *QILT Handbook* (1995) and *QILT Improvement Plans* (1995) are available from the QILT Unit, University of East London, Longbridge Road, Dagenham, Essex RM8 2AS

Chapter 8

Splitting the Atom of Education

Alastair Pearce

INTRODUCTION

Most higher education institutions in Britain use integrated award structures to deliver large proportions of their teaching programmes. This chapter will examine the characteristics of such structures, reflect on why they were invented, speculate on what will replace them in the future, and consider what the academic community should be doing in the final years of the 20th century to ensure the academic structures of the next century are as good as possible.

In this paper 'integrated award structures' refers to schemes of organizing programmes of study which typically share a single academic and regulatory structure comprising several courses leading to a variety of awards. They do not usually permit 'pick and mix' unit selection by students, but do facilitate the sharing of appropriate units by students on different, but often cognate, courses. The Credit Accumulation and Transfer Scheme (CATS) is usually used to decide progression and award.

Unless the world ends by the turn of the century, it is unlikely that integrated award structures will be judged the final expression of perfection in terms of academic organization. It is therefore important to plan for the future if the mistakes of the past are to be avoided. Integrated award structures were introduced as a reaction to changed external circumstances; the academic community failed to be proactive and simply did the best it could. A repeat of this process is unlikely to generate the best academic structures. The planning of the past tended to leave staff feeling powerless and sensing a creeping tide of inevitability in the introduction of change – this must also be avoided.

The future must therefore be planned. To do so it is necessary to look at what is now in place; to examine how the academic community arrived at this position (for the present may be a staging post on a clear route from the past allowing predictions to be made about the future); and to consider the constraints of the future. This examination will allow the community to take action now to ensure that the academic structures of the first decades of the 21st century are as good as they can be.

CHARACTERISTICS OF INTEGRATED AWARD STRUCTURES

Put somewhat crudely, current integrated award structures facilitate access through expanding student choice. On the negative side, staff and students can feel lost within the complexity and size of the structures, and academics still sometimes argue that there is a diminution of academic cohesion in that choice allows the study of groups of units not traditionally followed concurrently. The overall benefit of integrated award structures is that they allow a closer match between the students' personal educational requirements and the learning opportunities provided by the institution; the generally perceived loss centres on the size and aims of such structures causing administrative complexity resulting in students and staff losing a sense of territorial security.

WHY INTEGRATED AWARD STRUCTURES WERE INVENTED

Integrated award structures were born as a reaction to both a changing external environment and evolving ideas of education. The external pressures meant that institutions had to expand rapidly in terms of student numbers and consequently maximize the use of human and physical resources while minimizing financial costs. Educational ideas included a recognition that expansion implied an increase in the diversity of students' reasons to study and a concomitant realization that the immutable 'course' could not satisfy this need.

The knock-on effect of these pressures and solutions has seen academic staff learning large-group teaching techniques, accepting that students in a single lecture may be following a range of different courses in different modes, worrying about the external examiners' ability to cope, and reflecting on what is 'graduateness' in the UK.

For this degree of change to have been tolerated by the sector as a whole, there must have been a defensible academic credo giving it some justification. It was provided by the plausible assertion that the predefined, monolithic course of the past only satisfies the educational requirements of a certain number of today's students. These students are predominantly between 18 and 21 years old, have come up through conventional 'A' levels and wish to study full time for three consecutive years at one institution, and have the money to be able to do that. It is clear that a substantial, and growing, proportion of students are no longer like that. What the educational community has successfully done is to devise academic structures that start to cope with diversity of educational requirement. The structures facilitate part-time study, use CATS to promote mobility and non-consecutive study and allow greater flexibility in the choice of units making up a valid programme of study.

A clear historical development is taking place which is moving away from the prepackaged subject-based course that ignored diversity in students' educational requirements, and towards an acknowledgement, to some extent, of student diversity both in patterns of study and required academic content. However, the historical development has not yet reached its logical end-point, for our present structures merely *cope with* and *respond to* the changing educational environment, they still fail to *facilitate* and *lead* the way to better education. What is *better* in this sense? It is the extrapolation of the historical process here described: the closer match between students' diverse educational requirements and the educational opportunities institutions offer them. Although our current structures have taken the community in the right direction, the journey is not over.

WHAT ACADEMIC STRUCTURES WILL BE NEEDED IN THE FUTURE?

Although it is clearly impossible to predict the future with great hope of accuracy, the analysis of the past given above does indicate a consistent momentum towards the incorporation of certain identifiable attributes into future academic structures. It is impossible to define precisely what the structures will look like but it is possible (and vital) to divine what they must be able to do. The academic structure of the future must:

1. Help the student to analyse his or her outcomes of study
These are the student's personal reasons for studying. They may include career ambition, personal fulfilment and a host of other objective and subjective, cerebral and emotional elements. Without this analysis the partnership between student and institution cannot be confident that the education provided will be of any use.

2. Provide learning outcomes matched to each student's outcomes of study
Learning outcomes are the identifiable academic results of elements of study, generally *units* or *modules* in the last years of the 20th century. It is necessary for the student to know these before registering if he or she is to match them to his or her personal outcomes of study.

3. Promote quality of educational provision

4. Provide a community of study
This community may, of course, be a virtual, electronic community.

5. Facilitate flexible patterns of study
Typically allowing the student to study using a variety of different modes and intensities of attendance together with a combination of distance-learning styles.

6. Define the level of subject-specific skill and transferable skill for each learning outcome
The definition of 'graduateness' will have been further refined from the bottom up so that each learning outcome can be related to a commonly understood level through the identification of the skills likely to have been gained by the student.

7. Define awards as explicit collections of subject-specific and transferable skills achieved at defined levels
Following the previous point, awards can now be located both in terms of threshold level of achievement and as a definable collection of skills the holder must possess to receive the award.

8 Give value for money, be respected, auditable, transparent and easy to use
Apart from presenting requirements for the future, this list acknowledges and respects the interests of the seven key stakeholders: the students, the teaching staff, the administrative staff, funding bodies, auditing bodies, the employer, and the subject itself.

It is salutary to measure the success of current integrated award structures in meeting these eight requirements of the future – some are approached rather impressively, others are not addressed at all. Our current academic structures often make some attempt at the first through open days and perhaps APEL meetings, but these are generally skewed towards what the course has to offer rather than asking what the student needs. The second is currently left to the skill of the applicant to sort out. Arguably, existing integrated award structures achieve number three quite well. It is less certain that the fourth point is really met given the problems of sharing units of study. Although great progress has been made in meeting the fifth requirement, the choices are often full time *or* part time, distance leaning *or* attendance; flexible and changing combinations of study are far less likely to be available. Unit descriptions often address the sixth necessity well when describing subject-specific skills, but they tend to be more reticent on transferable skills.

Below the level of the unit, the identification of skills becomes more haphazard, they may be implied through the assessment criteria of a particular assignment but the student can often be left unsure what he or she is meant to gain from doing a specific piece of work. While some institutions define for their awards attainment levels (requirement seven) which cross discipline boundaries, this is not yet universal. Current integrated award structures probably do give *value for money* (requirement eight), the degree of respect they excite is less clear, they are certainly subject to frequent audit but their *transparency* and ease of use is debatable.

One key to achieving this list more successfully in the future is to consider the size of the 'atom of education' (the unit of study which seems difficult and unproductive to split, but when divided releases educational energy). Until the advent of integrated award structures, the atom of education used to be 'the course' – a single, but multifaceted, educational entity, based on a universal idea of what the subject was and what was needed to become a member of the community of the subject. The course delivered 'all you need to know' to join the subject community.

This atom of education has now, in many cases, been split into units or modules linked by integrated award structures. The educational energy released has resulted in eased access to elements of the discipline and greater precision in the definition of aims and objectives, content, assessment and learning outcomes. The current atom of education is the unit. What would happen if this were to be split?

The educational energy released by splitting the unit would allow different students on the same unit to be studying for different learning outcomes at different levels. The unit becomes a menu instead of 'today's special'.

Splitting the unit allows requirements two, six and seven to be approached, for learning outcomes now become more precisely associated with elements of study and these can be defined as providing appropriate subject-specific and transferable skills which contribute to the larger-scale collections that comprise awards. Additionally, the process of splitting the unit, with its associated sharpening of focus on learning outcomes, facilitates the matching of students' personal outcomes of study to the learning outcomes provided by the institution.

The very considerable downside of this proposed development is in increased complexity making the eighth requirement even harder to achieve. The problem is simple: lots of information will be required for lots of different purposes by lots of different people. Some of the more obvious information requirements are listed below.

The student needs to know:
- the learning outcomes available in the institution;
- how these might match his or her personal outcomes of study;
- the levels of the learning outcomes;

- the range of awards associated with different combinations of learning outcomes at different levels;
- how much the education will cost.

The institution needs to know:
- that the selected learning outcomes constitute a valid programme of study;
- which students are registered on which units for which learning outcomes;
- which learning outcomes have been successfully achieved;
- how much to charge the student.

The professional body/employer needs to know:
- what the graduate can and cannot do.

This degree of complexity and *need to know* cannot be met by current administrative systems. The splitting of the atom of education down to the learning outcome multiplies the complexity of administration many times. If this proposal is to work and be affordable the mundane data collection, organization and distribution of information must rely on institution-wide, computer-based systems rather than human beings.

The computer network must be able to support a student-centred expert system allowing coherent patterns of study to be selected. At the more detailed unit level the system will conduct the negotiation of required learning outcomes available from each unit. For example, the unit might lead to a range of five or six learning outcomes each associated with an assessment procedure. The computer system will allow the student to select the appropriate learning outcomes to help fulfil his or her personal outcomes of study, recognizing the pattern of assessment this will trigger and so meeting the first and second requirements listed above.

The system now knows the units to be taken and the learning outcomes to be claimed. It can therefore identify the award that will be gained by successfully completing the diet of work, for learning outcomes and institutional 'levels of attainment' are, arguably, comparable (fulfilling requirement seven). The system could also list evidence likely to constitute APEL (accreditation of prior experiential learning) exemption from agreed units with defined outcomes. The identification of financial cost to the student could follow, together with details of possible modes of study and timetable information. Payment having been guaranteed, the interactive registration process could end with the enrolment of the student onto elements of units comprising the negotiated and coherent pattern of work which fulfils his or her personal outcomes of study.

THE ACADEMIC STRUCTURES OF THE FUTURE

The academic community needs to be working now to ensure that the academic structures of the future serve the needs of their students. Many of the key features of the academic structure of the 21st century outlined here are already in existence, at least in embryo, in the final decade of the 20th century. What needs to be carried out is a detailed investigation of their potential followed by an analysis of the ways they can be combined into a single set of educational philosophies, regulatory procedures, physical networks, administrative working practices, and teaching and learning tools. Each of the main features already in existence is listed below.

Computer networks

An investigation should be made into the current use of university-wide networks which provide expert advice to students on available courses and units, and into those which facilitate registration of students onto programmes of study. This work will pave the way for the computer system of the new academic structure which will conduct student negotiation, and store and disseminate information associated with the registration process.

Units of study

Current experience of split units and normal, unsplit, units delivered simultaneously at different levels should be examined. An investigation of this kind will allow a greater understanding to be gained of the opportunities and problems associated with single educational units which address more than one learning outcome. This feature is central to the new academic structure in providing a wide range of learning outcomes helping the match between students' reasons for studying and the education provided by the institution to be as close as possible.

Graduateness

The investigation carried out into 'graduateness' by the Higher Education Quality Council is a valuable stepping stone to the future, because it promotes the clear definition of threshold skills achieved by students holding various awards. Through this approach, subject-specific and transferable skills can be made explicit and consequently matched to learning outcomes. The academic structure of the future needs this information to build appropriate combinations of learning outcomes into awards which fulfil the outcomes of study of the student, the audit requirements of internal and external agencies, and the interests of employers and professional bodies.

Negotiated study

Much needs to be learnt from current experience of programmes based on negotiated study. It is perhaps the case that such programmes tend to be viewed somewhat sceptically by staff and students more familiar with course-centred views of education. One possible explanation for this scepticism lies in the mystery of negotiation and the absence, in some cases, of clarity in the definition of the learning outcomes to be achieved. This issue must be addressed before the new academic structure can emerge, for it relies on the transparent mapping through negotiation of learning outcomes onto students' personal outcomes of study.

If these four actions can be completed before the century ends, they will prepare the ground not only for the future academic structure sketched here but also for a variety of alternative structures which share the conviction that the matching of a student's personal and desired outcomes of study to the educational opportunities offered by an institution is an important component in good teaching and learning.

The final years of the 20th century is an appropriate time for planning these developments in educational provision. The movement from elite through mass to possible universal higher education in Britain allows a laudable expansion of opportunity for students and prompts a much needed reassessment of the relationship between what is taught and what is needed to be taught. Combined with this evolution in educational philosophy is the newly available university-wide computer network which can absorb much of the administrative impact of changes caused by the movement away from elite higher education. The confluence of educational philosophy and technical availability is a lucky accident which should allow the academic community to plan and create the future rather than simply twitch in passive response to changing external political and financial pressures.

Chapter 9

Developing HE Staff to Appreciate the Needs of Flexible Learning Access Students – Developing Flexible Learning Access Students to Appreciate the Needs of HE

Sally Anderson and Fred Percival

INTRODUCTION

The use of more flexible delivery systems has particular relevance for certain groups of learners for whom traditional attendance is not appropriate. Napier University has been running two innovative projects using flexible / distance delivery to make university entry a possibility for two of these groups: those completing qualifications in the FE sector and those who do not have traditionally accepted qualifications, particularly the unemployed.

This chapter briefly describes the two projects, and then focuses on how they have encouraged staff to reassess their attitudes towards 'acceptable' qualifications, prior experiential learning and the knowledge and skill requirements for university access; and how students have been oriented to study in a university context.

THE PROJECTS

Flexible learning bridging course scheme

This project's aim was to develop accelerated entry opportunities for further education students into university degree courses. It was funded by the Scottish Higher Education Funding Council (SHEFC) under the first round of funding in their Flexibility in Teaching and Learning Scheme (FITLS). The main objective of the project was to offer bridging courses to enable students on HNC and HND courses in selected disciplines (Engineering and Business Administration in the pilot) to gain entry at Levels 2 and 3 respectively of existing undergraduate degrees offered at Napier University. The idea was to look at the syllabi covered in the HNC or HND, and to look at what students would need to be able to do in the year of the university course they went into. Any gaps identified would be made up in the bridging course, which would also prepare students for more independent learning and a move away from competence-based approaches.

It was decided that these courses should be offered in flexible learning mode because it allowed students to complete them over a period that suited them. In addition, it was felt that flexible learning would allow students to develop useful study skills and attitudes in preparation for university. It was also felt that material created for the bridging course would have wider application, and producing it as print-based, flexible learning study guides would facilitate that. In the end, it was anticipated that a bank of materials in various subjects would be available for use in a variety of combinations.

Accordingly, in the Engineering area, materials were developed for foundation maths, foundation electrical, statistics, calculus, algebra, manufacturing systems, thermodynamics, and design process. In Business Administration, material was developed for financial reporting, macro-economic policy and economics of firms, industry and competition. Two generic modules called 'Effective Learning' and 'Information Sources' were also produced. The idea was that every student would follow a particular programme based on their particular bridging needs, but that all students would do the two generic subjects.

As the project was collaborative between Napier University, Perth College and Falkirk College, it was decided to pilot the scheme in two areas where students of the colleges might have a particular desire to go on to university study, and also where an appropriate knowledge base meant that the bridge would not have to be unmanageably large: Engineering and Business Administration. However, it is interesting to note that the *concept* of a bridging course was validated by the university, rather than the specific pilot schemes. This is the first time that the university has formally validated bridging arrangements into courses.

With regard to student support and tutoring, the project works on the basis that students will be supported by tutors at the further education college, who will also administer assessments and mark them as well as coursework. Coursework would be monitored on a sample basis by Napier course leaders, and all assessments would be checked by them. The first students were taken on in May.

Enhancement course

This course was designed to improve access to higher education for disadvantaged groups, in particular the unemployed. It was funded by

SHEFC as part of the second round of Flexibility in Teaching and Learning Scheme projects. The idea here was to provide a route into diploma and degree courses in science and engineering for those who did not necessarily have formal, traditional qualifications for entry. This was achieved through a combination of flexible learning materials and summer schools.

Flexible learning was chosen as the appropriate study mode in this case, not only because it helped to develop skills needed for further study and is often the preferred mode for adults who have many demands on their time, but also because it allowed those unemployed candidates who are capable of, available for, and actively seeking work, to continue to receive unemployment benefit while enrolled. Three courses were identified by the collaborating institutions as being essential groundwork for entry into the science and engineering fields of study. They were: Mathematics, Science and Learning Strategies.

Through a programme of self-profiling and counselling, potential participants are directed towards at least one of the enhancement courses. They then study the appropriate flexible learning materials, receiving assistance from a tutor based at the university and submitting assignments for marking and feedback. Their summative assessment is taken at the completion of a two-week summer school.

PREPARING STAFF

The obvious initial area common to both these projects was in helping staff to write flexible learning materials. This training took on added importance because of the non-traditional, and often disadvantaged nature of the students. This meant that the authors were being asked to write in a far less formal way than usual. (Just getting some members of academic staff to use the first person in writing is a struggle.) Besides this, each project had some particular aspects which threw up interesting implications for staff.

Bridging course

A difficulty here was to get subject experts to take a dispassionate look at what students were covering and decide which parts were absolutely essential grounding, and which were additional input. The initial reaction, of course, was 'but everyone must have everything'. This was particularly true in the Engineering field, and the list of subjects developed for that bridging course gives evidence of that. There was no instant resolution of this difficulty, and it is still being worked on. However, much discussion has helped, and it is hoped that as students move through the bridging course and into degree courses, their success will convince the doubting Thomases.

It was also recognized that tutors at the colleges would have to provide bridging course students with substantial support in light of the fact that they were carrying a significantly increased load in some cases (their final year of HNC or HND as well as the bridging course). They also needed some training in marking flexible learning assignments: how to provide feedback, how the students might feel while studying in this manner, and so on. Meetings were held to explore these issues. An open communication channel was also maintained between tutors and the flexible learning unit at Napier, so that problems could be dealt with as they arose.

Members of the departments that students join are kept up to date on their progress, so that the transition to the degree can be made as smooth as possible. Faculty advisers find that they need to be prepared to provide extra help to students who join an established class at this late stage.

Enhancement course

Here staff concerns centred on reaction to the fact that many students might have little in the way of formal qualifications. It was difficult to separate maintaining standards from entry requirements. Issues such as APEL had to be explored in some depth, as the feeling was often that if the student had no Highers (Higher School Certificates), he or she had 'nothing'. Quite a bit of mediation was necessary during these discussions to keep them amicable! A very positive factor was that some non-traditional entry students of a similar background were now in year two of various courses and doing well.

Part of the discomfort about these students related to the fact that they might need special counselling and guidance at all stages of the enhancement course, as well as during the first year of their degree course. To alleviate this concern, advisors were trained in a seminar/workshop with staff from the Open University who have considerable experience in dealing with students from non-traditional backgrounds.

Mature students are often under pressure as the only ones in the class with 'life experience'. They may also be more comfortable asking for lots of help. Circumstances like these can mean that lecturers and course leaders become involved in providing more support than they are used to. It was therefore noted that lecturers should be given a full profile of students who enter through the enhancement course route, so that they are fully aware of the circumstances before classes get under way.

The discussions above point to some degree of resistance from staff to exploring options for taking in students from non-traditional backgrounds. However, this resistance is less and less visible as the fear of under-recruitment, with all its consequences, becomes a factor. This is balanced by a need to avoid a high drop-out rate, so that not only are departments more prepared to consider such candidates, they are also more prepared to put in place the support mechanisms that give them a reasonable chance of success.

PREPARING STUDENTS

Bridging course

A primary concern here was to help students to become accustomed to a more independent way of studying, and to prepare them for examination-type summative assessment. The primary means of doing this was the use of two subjects – Effective Learning, and Information Sources – which all students had to complete as the first two areas of study in their bridging course. Among areas covered, Effective Learning assists students in setting up achievable goals and timetables for completing the work. Information Sources is designed to familiarize students with resource-based work, and has a number of projects that require intensive use of library facilities.

Various assessment methods have been used throughout the course. The two subjects mentioned are assessed by portfolio and project respectively. However, the more formal subjects are assessed under examination conditions. This was essential to prepare students for university assessment. Feedback from students indicates that, despite efforts to explain this strategy, they were not fully prepared for examinations, and more support and explanation about this needs to be given.

It is difficult for students who have come through this route to fit into their degree courses, as they are 'new' but are not placed in the first year, and consideration is being given to special induction programmes for them. However, numbers so far have been too small to make this practical.

Enhancement course

The most interesting challenge in relation to preparing students from the unemployed group for university was to encourage them to consider further or higher education as an option in the first place. In order to do this without undue pressure, they were provided with a self-profiling tool which they could complete for their own use. If they wished they could send the completed questionnaire in with their application form, but they did not have to do so. This tool guided the student through a series of questions about motivation, work experience, personal goals, and so on. It was found that even this proved to be a daunting prospect for some potential students, and a series of follow-up mechanisms has been put in place to encourage them to complete the self-profiling tool, and then to take the next step and come in for an interview.

Once enrolled on the enhancement course, students have a variety of support mechanisms available, and do well. Much like the bridging course, it contains a subject called Learning Strategies, which is designed not only to introduce students to the concept of studying by flexible learning, but also to assist them to plan achievable study goals and manage their time effectively. The summer school (a two-week intensive face-to-face session just before the start of the academic year) provides an opportunity to sort out problems encountered during independent study. At the end of the school, students take formal assessments for Mathematics and Science. Learning Strategies is assessed by portfolio. Once again, this is excellent preparation for the assessment methods of subsequent university courses. Feedback has been encouraging, and a number of students are now enrolled on degree or diploma courses.

Chapter 10

Managing to Help Teachers Change: An Agenda for Academic Managers

Barry Jackson

INTRODUCTION: AN AGENDA

There is considerable pressure to change teaching and learning methods in higher education. Most of this pressure is perceived to be externally imposed, arising from the increasing number and diversity of students, and a reduction in resources. There is also, in some quarters, a perception that change is needed, intrinsically, in order to improve the quality of students' learning regardless of the externally imposed agenda.

Many institutional missions now formally recognize the need for changes in teaching and learning (although this appears to be predominantly related to the externally imposed agenda). Some institutions have stressed the value they place on teaching by implementing promotion schemes for excellent teachers. As a consequence there has been a good deal of educational and staff development activity. It is no longer difficult for most teaching staff to find advice and help on educational development issues, or to develop their teaching skills, should they wish. Many, however, appear to be reluctant to take these opportunities. The best efforts of staff and educational developers can fail to overcome a resistance to change.

The strength of this resistance is rooted in the nature of academics' self-perception, their perception of institutional priorities, and in the culture of academic departments. Academics are given little real encouragement to change their view of their proper role, and they are not confident that teaching is valued as highly as research, in spite of institutional mission statements. There is some evidence to support their view.

In this context, academic managers have a particular and critical role, which has not been adequately addressed. It is a manager's responsibility to encourage and support colleagues' adaptation to change: doing so is a difficult task. The nature of the academic context means that models of organizational change and staff development that have their origins in industrial contexts may not be appropriate. Other models, based on the strengths of academic practices, should be sought. There is a need for senior academic managers to be centrally involved in this. Determining and delivering a more effective, context-dependent programme of change management will require the active participation of senior managers. A significant implication of this analysis is that the most urgent priority group for staff development is senior management!

There are a number of ways in which managers may approach the task of encouraging colleagues to change, and some principles and approaches are suggested below.

THE NATURE OF AND REASONS FOR CHANGE

Why do teachers need to change? For anyone working outside higher education the answers may not yet be obvious. For those employed in higher education in the late 1990s the question is answered daily by the experiences of teachers trying to maintain the quality of what they do, using methodologies and assumptions that were developed in a different time, for a different kind of educational system. Transformation of the higher education system is likely to continue, increasing the urgency for change.

Recent changes in the world of higher education, principally brought about by the 1988 Education Reform Act and the 1992 Further and Higher Education Act, have been substantial. Significant changes have occurred in the funding, direction and mission of higher education, all of which have an impact on the teaching of students, and therefore on their learning. Many of the problems facing higher education have arisen from the friction between an emerging mass education system and the elite values which characterize traditional academic organizations. Reducing resources have worsened the ratio of students to staff, while at the same time institutions are diverting resources to the development of learning resource provision to enable distance and open learning.

Structural changes have introduced elements of modularity and/or semesterization into most institutions (over half according to a 1994 CVCP survey), with consequent compartmentalization of the curriculum and increased emphasis on assessment. The structural changes have partly succeeded in one of their aims, which was to open the experience of higher education to a wider variety of students. Now students with a greater variety of abilities and backgrounds are entering higher education, in a greater variety of modes of attendance. These students are entering a system largely evolved to meet the needs of a small number of mainly middle-class 18–21 year olds with traditional 'A' level attainment, studying in uninterrupted full-time mode.

Accompanying these structural changes during the 1990s there has been a change in the organizational image of higher education. Davies (1987) has described the change as being from the 'Providing' tradition, whose dominant metaphors are: Collegiality, Bureaucracy, Organized Anarchy to the 'Client/Consumer' tradition, with the dominant metaphors of Consumerism, Business and Public Accountability. This change is one that allows little space for the intimate, self-determining culture of traditional collegial values, and it has done little to warm the hearts of academics.

During the same period there have been changing perceptions of learning and teaching. Developing technologies of information storage, com-munication and retrieval are having an impact on teaching strategies, and are increasingly prominent in institutional and government priorities, as indicated by the Teaching and Learning Technology initiative. Alongside technological development there has been a slow but incremental spread of ideas founded on the research into learning which began in the 1970s with the work of Marton, Säljö, Entwistle and others, and which has now pervaded corners of every discipline and most institutions. The period has seen a rise in the number of publications, in book, journal and electronic form, dedicated to the analysis of current teaching practices and the development of improved ones. Ironically, a more general recognition of the need to improve university teaching has just begun to emerge, as a severe resource reduction, which makes it imperative to change, makes change more difficult.

In this context, it should not be forgotten that there is, and always has been, an intrinsic impetus to change, to which some teachers at least are susceptible. This is the teacher's own recognition of the need for, or value of, improvement. It has been described as a natural part of the good teacher's practice. There is evidence that good practice of this kind is spread throughout the sector, but in pockets.

Given the external pressures for change, as well as the determination of some colleagues to improve their own practice, it is perhaps surprising that changes in teaching strategies have not moved very far overall. Although pockets of innovative practice exist, there is no evidence of a thorough revision of teaching methods going on. We might question the reasons for this: some of them may lie in the characteristics and perceptions of academic staff discussed next.

CHARACTERISTICS OF ACADEMIC STAFF

In many ways, higher education retains its collegial nature: the staff view their relationship to their employer and to the responsibilities of the job in ways that are quite different to those in most occupations. Staff see themselves as autonomous, self-managed, subject experts. This view occasionally finds public utterance, as in this quote from a letter by a university lecturer to the *Guardian* in 1991:

> 'I do not wish to be a teacher, I am employed as a lecturer and in my naiveté I thought my job was to "know" my field, contribute to it by research and to lecture on my specialism! Students attend my lectures but the onus to learn is on them. It is not my job to teach them.' (quoted in Evans, 1993)

The traditions of academe encourage staff to value highly their individual expertise and knowledge, and at the same time to challenge authority. It is a minority of lecturers whose teaching practices have been informed by serious or certificated study of learning and teaching.

CHARACTERISTICS OF ACADEMIC MANAGERS

Most academic managers, heads of department or deans of faculty, are academics, and have progressed through similar experiences and structures as other academics. It is not surprising to discover that managers share many characteristics with other academic staff. For some this creates a certain tension, as they struggle to reconcile being in authority with a sense that authority should rightly be challenged. There is a view shared by teachers and managers that authority is never permanent and must always be defended by rational argument. As Middlehurst (1993) has noted, 'Leadership (in academe) is defined by the ability to convince and persuade others to act on the basis of greater knowledge or competence, reasoned argument and fairness'. Middlehurst provides some examples of statements by heads of department which illustrate this tension:

> 'Leadership means having the authority and status to impose one's views on the department and know that the department accepts you as a leader because you are who you are.... Heads of department in universities have no effective managerial power and operate by inspiring or engineering consent.'

SUPPORT FOR CHANGE

There are a number of ways in which change is supported, and encouraged, both within and outside of institutions. Various agents of change, and sources of support for those who wish to see change can be identified. These may include staff and educational developers, colleagues and managers.

There is also external support from agencies such as Higher Education Quality Council Division of Quality Enhancement, the Staff and Educational Development Association (SEDA) and external development providers, such as the Oxford Centre for Staff Development (OCSD). These external agencies, by keeping up a presence and encouraging networks of developing change and innovation, provide a less threatening external pressure than other external forces. Nonetheless, the threat of Funding Council teaching quality assessments acts as its own powerful encouragement to institutions to reflect on their teaching practices.

OBSTACLES TO CHANGE – THE 3Rs

The biggest obstacles to change in academic organizations can conveniently be classified as the three 'Rs': Research culture; Resistance to management; Reluctance to train.

Research culture

It is certain that the pressure to increase research outweighs the pressure to improve teaching. This is in spite of an increase in the rhetoric of university mission statements expressing a commitment to recognize the value of good teaching. A survey in 1995 of all 145 UK higher education institutions (Gibbs, 1995) found that:

- almost all included excellence in teaching as a criterion for promotion;
- only one in ten promotions actually were for excellence in teaching;
- four in ten institutions had promoted nobody on the grounds of excellence in teaching.

For some academic staff this, of course, merely reflects how it ought to be: in their view, subject experts, after all, should be rewarded more than teachers. But others who may not be so fixed in their perceptions regarding the nature of the academic's job will see little to encourage them to prioritize the development of their teaching rather than their research skills.

The research culture in UK universities has seen significant growth during the mid-1990s, particularly in connection with the aim of new universities, traditionally institutions that valued teaching over research, to demonstrate their new research strength in the 1996 Research Assessment Exercise. There is little doubt that this new alignment of priorities is welcomed by many staff, whose inclination is to value research more highly than teaching anyway.

Resistance to management

We have hinted above at the difficulties academics have in seeing themselves as managers, and particularly, as leaders. To lead staff in a strategic way requires that the leader forgo some of the academic, collegial values with which he or she has grown up. The difficulty is compounded by the attitudes of teaching staff, who may not accept that any authority has validity. As one head has remarked, 'many academics do not see themselves as belonging to a structure that has to be managed at all' (Middlehurst 1993).

It may not be surprising that a survey of teaching staff in Australian universities (Moses and Roe, 1990) found that staff believed that the most important function of the head of department was to serve as an advocate of the department. The second most important function was to consider staff views. The development of strategic plans for the department was not considered to warrant higher than third place.

Leadership seems to be particularly problematic in academic organizations. Kerr and Jermier (1978) noted that in some organizations there are elements that may substitute or neutralize leadership, rendering leadership ineffective. Middlehurst summarizes the nature of these elements:

'Substitutes render the leader's behaviour redundant or unnecessary; these variables might include the nature of the task (which may be intrinsically motivating), the characteristics of the followers (perhaps autonomous professionals) or the structures and norms of the organisation (where roles are clear and communication operates freely). Neutralisers, on the other hand, prevent the leader from acting in particular ways or counteract the effects of leadership; these might include lack of control over rewards, the competence and training of subordinates, inflexible organisational policies or procedures.' (1993, p.25)

It is easy to see that the academic environment can provide many 'substitutes' and 'neutralizers' for leadership.

Reluctance to train

Academics do not demonstrate an appetite for training. It might appear odd that a profession that is based on teaching appears to distrust the teaching of others. There can be a number of reasons for this, which Middlehurst (1993) has elaborated in a description of the 'academic cults' that underlie resistance to leadership training. The same cults might be seen as affecting academic views of any training, including teaching training. Indeed, some of the views summarized in the list below I have heard used in relation to the teaching of students themselves:

• **The cult of the gifted amateur** (any intelligent, educated individual can undertake the task, without training).

- **The cult of heredity** (those with natural talent will emerge since they are born to the task).
- **The cult of deficiency** (training is essentially remedial or for those who are personally ineffective – 'training is for the second eleven' as one Pro-Vice-Chancellor put it).
- **The cult of inadequacy** (once qualified, loss of face is involved by admitting gaps in one's knowledge or competence).
- **The cult of the implicit** (development takes place by gradual induction into the norms and operations of academe; learning by osmosis is the hallmark of success).
- **The cult of selection** (the selection of good staff will ensure good performance and will obviate the need for – and the cost of – development).
- **The cult of the intellectual** (there is no scientific basis to 'management', therefore it does not deserve to be taken seriously).

The fourth R

A fourth R acts both as a stimulus and an obstacle to change, and that is Resources. The lack of sufficient resources is frequently raised as an obstacle to change or as a reason for not undertaking staff development or for not investigating one's own practice, and yet it is the need to adapt to a declining unit of resource that would appear to be driving, in exasperation, the greatest amount of change.

TOWARDS SOLUTIONS

Starting point – working with academic culture

The starting point in moving towards workable solutions must be a recognition of the importance of changing conceptions as well as behaviours. To simply change behaviours needs continual monitoring and control. Constant control takes up too much of managers' time. It also allows no autonomy to the teacher, and this conflicts with the values of academe, as we have argued above, in which individual responsibility is valued highly. It is likely therefore to undermine the sense of involvement needed for effective transformation.

Much of the staff development on offer to academics appears to be inappropriately based on models derived from industry. The skill or technique-based workshop, provided by a central staff development service, is often very effective with administrative staff but worthless with teaching staff. It is time to recognize that another approach should be taken. Staff development needs to work with the characteristics of academic culture if it is to be effective. Gibbs has pointed out that this approach is increasingly taken in America. Here a strong research culture is being used to develop teaching: 'the research elite are harnessing what they are good at to improve what they have not been so good at' (Gibbs, 1995).

The potential of managers in change

In spite of the resistance to management outlined above, the academic manager role is one with considerable potential for the encouragement of change. Unlike staff development units, the academic manager generally comes from within the subject discipline of their colleagues, and consequently carries a certain credibility among colleagues. She or he also carries a certain amount of authority – a good leader will be able to make clear where the boundaries of acceptable responses lie – without encouraging a purely compliance culture. Moses (1985) indicates a range of manager actions that are likely to contribute to a climate of excellence in teaching:

- regular discussions of teaching and the curriculum;
- regular evaluation of teaching;
- resources allocated to teaching;
- praise and promotion recommendations for good teaching;
- support for innovation and development;
- encouragement of interdisciplinary teaching.

The potential of management involvement in change can go beyond this good practice, however. If managers recognize that their principal role is one of 'transformation' they may come to see themselves more as academic leaders rather than simply administrative managers. Leaders can help their colleagues to change in several ways, sharing with them the difficult tasks of letting go of some aspects of practice in order to explore new ones. It is important that both managers and teachers learn to do things differently, but it is the manager's responsibility to provide the cognitive frameworks within which this can happen.

The leader's task can be seen as analogous to the teacher's. The teacher's role is to facilitate students in undertaking a deep approach to learning, in order to transform their understanding. The leader's role is to help staff to transform their own understanding, which requires a similar deep approach. It is a matter of learning, of developing greater cognitive complexity.

Models of change

The potential of leadership intervention in helping teachers to change can be developed in several ways:

- Managers can encourage change by structuring opportunities for staff to be exposed to new approaches, so that they are 'experiencing things from a variety of viewpoints, in order to understand that one has a viewpoint' (Marton 1995).

- Managers can be guides to action research: explaining, supporting and collaborating with their staff in action research, evaluating and improving teaching practice. The experienced manager can help colleagues in the reflection and appraisal of their teaching practice. Action research is a powerful model: although its primary purpose is the improvement of practice, it can readily be reported on, leading to 'research outcomes' which are acceptable in the more traditional sense of research. Some academic colleagues will find this a more credible form of staff development than that offered by workshops on teaching and learning. The potential for educational action research has been explored by Zuber-Skerritt (1992).

- Action learning can provide a means of group support and development which managers can offer to colleagues. Action learning groups can be very helpful in providing anxiety-free situations in which staff can discuss their own progress in developing teaching in a structured way. They are well described in McGill and Beaty (1995).

- A valuable approach to helping staff to change may be taken by managers who are aware of the research and theoretical frameworks which currently inform thinking about student learning. Just as teachers can use these frameworks to help them design and deliver learning situations that will encourage a deep approach to learning, so managers can use them to encourage a deep approach to learning in their staff. Deep approaches bring about changed conceptions: if teachers are to really change their practices, they will need to change their conceptions. The research and theoretical background is introduced in Gibbs (1992).

What becomes clear is that few of the proposals listed here could be effective without the support of experienced, trained managers who have a well developed understanding of the issues and of the processes involved. Staff development efforts may be better targeted at management staff, since there is no evidence that academic managers as a whole demonstrate the qualities required. Staff development for academic managers needs to be carefully designed, and built on appropriate models – those of leadership writers in non-academic organizations will simply not work. It may be that the cheapest and most effective way of bringing about change in teaching practices is to change the managers into academic leaders.

REFERENCES

Davies, J L (1987) 'The Entrepreneurial and Adaptive University: Report of the Second US Study Visit', *International Journal of Institutional Management*, **11**, 1, 12–104.

Evans, C (1993) *English People: The Experience of Teaching and Learning English in British Universities*, Open University Press, Milton Keynes.

Gibbs, G (1992) *Improving the Quality of Student Learning*, Technical and Educational Services, Plymouth.

Gibbs, G (1995) 'Models of Staff Development', *The New Academic*, **4**, 3, 15–17.

Kerr, S and Jermier, J M (1978) 'Substitutes for Leadership: Their Meaning and Measurement', *Organizational Behaviour and Human Performance*, **22**, 375–403.

Marton, F (1995) Lecture delivered at Improving Student Learning Symposium, Exeter, 1995 (in publication).

McGill, I and Beaty, L (1995) *Action Learning: A Guide for Professional, Management and Educational Development*, 2nd edn, Kogan Page, London.

Middlehurst, R (1993) *Leading Academics*, SRHE and Open University Press, Buckingham.

Moses, I (1985) 'The Role of the Head of Department in the Pursuit of Excellence', *Higher Education*, **14**, 337–54.

Moses, I and Roe, E (1990) *Heads and Chairs: Managing Academic Departments*, University of Queensland Press, Brisbane.

Zuber-Skerritt, O (1992) *Professional Development in Higher Education: A Theoretical Framework for Action Research*, Kogan Page, London.

SECTION III
Responding to Changes in the Student Body

Chapter 11

Dissertation Supervision: Managing the Student Experience

Steve Armstrong

INTRODUCTION

Since the number of higher education students has trebled and become less homogeneous in recent years, new strategies are called for as staff resources have not changed proportionately. Significant research has been done into teaching and learning, but one facet still seriously overlooked is research or project supervision. As Acker *et al.* (1994) point out, research on thesis supervision has been little studied, despite numerous testimonies to its critical importance and exceptional difficulty, while Brown and Atkins (1988) suggest that research supervision is 'the most complex and subtle form of teaching in which we engage'.

This chapter describes an alternative model developed in the Business School of the University of Sunderland for the better management of the supervision of large groups of students undertaking final-year undergraduate research projects and compares it with more traditional methods. The core of the model is a surgery system involving 12 members of staff and 240 students. First-year results suggested that despite an increase of more than 25% in student numbers there was a manifest improvement in the quality of students' work compared with previous years. The most significant difference was in the number of students failing (3%) compared with the previous year (8%) when traditional methods of project supervision were used. Furthermore, the number of first-class projects increased from 7% to 15%, while the staff supervision hours were halved. All dissertations were double marked. When interviewed, students welcomed the opportunity for guaranteed and regular dialogue with their personal supervisors and attendance rates were higher (77% in the first semester). Overall, the system ensures structure, control and consistency throughout the supervisory team, which in turn results in less 'fire-fighting' at the end of the academic year.

In a survey involving 85 research students, Egglestone and Delamont (1983) found that the most frequent problem reported by students was their sense of isolation. The frequency (rather than length) of meetings is a significant factor in reducing this. An important feature of the Sunderland system is that each student is guaranteed a regular 20-minute appointment with the same supervisor on alternate weeks throughout the academic year.

In Rudd's study (1985) into postgraduate failure 20–25% of the students said they were 'seriously dissatisfied' with the supervision they received, yet Katz and Hartnett (1976) found that the relationship with supervisors was regarded by most graduate students as the single most important aspect of the quality of their research experience. In recent studies, Hill *et al.* (1994) also found that most relevant literature cites the critical influence of the student/supervisor relationship on completion rates. This raises the question of whether it is not more important to match the work styles of supervisors and students rather than matching by subject discipline. This view is supported by Philips and Pugh (1994) who suggest that provided the student has access to others expert in the area, it may be more important that the supervisor's style of work coincides with the student's.

This chapter also discusses current research into interpersonal dyad relationships which seeks to investigate the significance of matching students and supervisors according to their styles.

TRADITIONAL MODEL OF SUPERVISION

Within the University of Sunderland Business School traditional supervision methods were previously employed for both undergraduate final-year and postgraduate research projects. Each student had a named supervisor and the two were expected to cooperate in developing a dissertation or thesis. There were no formal controls in place to manage this supervision.

The number of undergraduate students in the Business School involved in this process has increased substantially in recent years. For example, students undertaking a final-year BA project in Business Administration rose from approximately 160 in 1993/94 to 212 in 1994/95, an increase of more than 25%; and in 1995/96 this figure rose by a further 18% to 250. This trend may well be compounded in future years by the increase in numbers of higher education students, a rise predicted to continue for the remainder of the decade.

Each Sunderland student is required to undertake a major project during his or her final year which is problem-solving in nature and related to a live business issue. The purpose is to give the student an opportunity to do assessed work demanding individual research, analysis of a problem and synthesis and evaluation of solutions. It also gives the student an opportunity to produce something that might benefit the 'real' world while simultaneously integrating many of the subjects covered in the student's course into one cohesive piece of work. This major project culminates in an 8,000 word dissertation and carries a value of 20 CATS points. The student is expected to spend a minimum of 150 hours on the project over a two-semester period spanning 30 teaching weeks.

The traditional supervision process for these undergraduate students became increasingly difficult to manage. It was expensive in terms of staff time and results from 20 interviews with students and staff suggested that the student experience was poor. Each supervisor would typically be responsible for five or six undergraduate student projects. The number of supervisors required would need to increase from 30 to about 50 using this traditional model and the cost in staff time would rise from 1,600 hours in 1993/94 to 2,500 hours in 1995/96 – equivalent to more than four full-time members of staff.

The dearth of formal controls under the traditional system increased the problems of managing a module of this complexity which led to significantly more complaints from both students and staff. A common one from students was that they found it increasingly difficult to organize meetings with their supervisors, while staff complained that students would not maintain contact and that dissertations would suddenly arrive at the end of the academic year, often when too late to consider any re-working. The quality of the dissertations was generally considered to have been low.

This unstructured approach to project supervision was deemed to be inappropriate in the academic year 1993/94, a view supported by other studies (eg, Rudd, 1985), which report lack of structure to be a common weakness in supervision. In order to improve the student experience, the quality of learning and the efficiency of the supervision process, it was decided that an alternative model of supervision was needed and that this should be piloted on the undergraduate programme described, within the Business School.

AN ALTERNATIVE MODEL

Wright and Lodwick (1989), in a study involving first-year postgraduate research students, concluded that 'at present, insufficient attention is paid to planning and programming the work, setting and keeping to deadlines'.

A new approach addressing these issues was developed and first implemented in the academic year 1994/95. At its core is a surgery system in which a team of staff meets with students in a common area on a weekly basis, on a strict appointment schedule. During its first year, 12 members of the newly appointed staff team each had 20-minute appointments between 2pm and 5.20pm on Monday afternoons. The students – 212 in all – were divided into two groups who were then seen on a one-to-one basis on alternate Mondays at specific times. Although these meetings are of short duration, the system guarantees a high frequency of meetings, which has been deemed to be more important than longer, infrequent ones (Cottrell *et al.*, 1994).

Operating procedures ensure that the various stages leading to the development of the 8,000-word dissertation are well controlled. For example, a year calendar with defined milestones is published in the students' handbook and staff adhere rigidly to these time scales. A record is made of each supervision meeting and a set of actions agreed for the next meeting. Both summative and formative assessments take place throughout the year, to help sustain student motivation. At the first supervision meeting each student is given a copy of the handbook and the 20-minute meeting is then spent carefully taking the student through its contents. This document pointedly differentiates the research project from the types of assignments developed through the student's previous two years of study. A strong emphasis is placed on the need for primary research and guidance is given on topic selection, literature searching, project planning, research methods, structure and presentation of the written report, methods of assessment, attendance requirements, the role of the supervisor (which is essentially a contract between student and supervisor) and especially the project calendar showing key milestones. A dissertation proposal form is also issued at this first meeting and the student is instructed to develop a suitable proposal through discussion with a chosen company and his or her academic supervisor.

The dissertation proposal is developed to a point at which the chosen organization is satisfied as to its usefulness and the academic supervisor considers it to be manageable within the allotted time scales and of appropriate academic worth. The proposal form, which defines the project title, issues to be investigated, possible research methods and a few related references, is approved in week 7/8. A project plan mapping out the journey through to project completion is submitted for discussion in week 5/6. A formal review is held in week 13/14 which is summatively assessed and contributes up to 10% of the student's final mark. At this review the supervisor assesses how well the student is controlling his or her project. To assist the supervisor in this task, students are expected to 'walk through' the contents of their project files and are also asked to submit a 200-word synopsis of progress at this meeting. Progress is reviewed against the following criteria:

- overall progress to date;
- timely and relevant dissertation proposal received;
- degree of project planning and management undertaken;
- actions set during weekly project meetings being satisfied;
- evidence of primary and/or secondary research.

The results of this review are made available to the student at the next supervision meeting. A draft dissertation is submitted for comment in week 21/22 and final submission is required in week 24/25. Individual vivae take place in weeks 29 and 30, further details of which are given below.
NB: Each half of the student cohort is seen on alternate weeks. The milestones therefore apply to odd and even weeks which are indicated above as week 1/2, 3/4 etc.

While the scheme described is highly structured with regard to controlling the research process, supervisors are careful not to be too directive about the content of the research. As Hill *et al.* (1994) point out, supervisors often de-emphasize direction because they are concerned not to destroy the creative process through imposing a rigid schema.

METHOD OF ASSESSMENT

Each project is assessed according to the following criteria.

- **Control (20%)** – awarded for demonstrating the ability to plan, monitor and control a working schedule throughout the duration of the project. This is divided into two parts, half of the marks being awarded at the formal review in weeks 13/14 as discussed above and the remainder at the end of the project.
- **Content (40%)** – awarded for the quality of research and analysis undertaken and the initiative in finding sources of information.
- **Dissertation (30%)** – awarded for the quality and clarity of the final written dissertation.
- **Viva (10%)** – awarded for the ability of the student to verbally communicate his or her conduct of the project and command over its subject area. In some cases the viva can also affect the marks awarded for control and content, although this is unlikely.

All dissertations are second marked (blind). The viva is conducted with the student's academic supervisor and second marker present.

RESULTING BENEFITS

When interviewed at the end of the first year of operation, many students expressed appreciation for the opportunity of guaranteed and regular dialogue with individual supervisors. For this particular student cohort there was no personal tutor support system in place, although several students claimed that this was a useful by-product of the process.

As stated earlier, the results for the 1994/95 academic year indicate that despite an increase of more than 25% in student numbers, the quality of work had been enhanced. The current scheme virtually guarantees regular contact between supervisor and student, which in turn ensures that the entire student experience is efficiently managed and results imply that the overall quality of the learning process has been enhanced.

The number of staff hours required has been reduced by a factor of two by adopting this new model – from 2,500 hours to 1,250 hours in the academic year 1995/96. Time spent fire-fighting problems at the end of the academic year was also reduced. While the logistics of organizing such a scheme are initially fairly complex, once under way the tendency has been for the process to run smoothly. The supervision system is also more easily managed due to substantially fewer staff being involved.

There are now over 2,000 students at the university undertaking research projects similar to those in the Business School. Methods of project supervision in the other schools have hitherto been mainly traditional and the problems reported by them are frequently similar to those previously experienced in the Business School. Clearly, it would be beneficial to both students and schools if alternative models were developed within those schools to deal more effectively and efficiently with the increasing student population, and the university is currently working towards introducing the new model of research/project supervision across these other schools. It is hoped that the pilot work outlined above will assist in the development of similar systems elsewhere.

CONTENT VERSUS PROCESS

When the new model was introduced, students were asked to state in which preferred subject areas they wished to base their projects (eg, Marketing, Economics, Finance) to facilitate provision of a staff team whose discipline profiles would align closely with the requirements of the student cohort. This student/tutor match was largely achieved in terms of subject discipline, which meant that both the *content* and the *process* of the research could be managed effectively for each student.

In a few cases such a match was not achieved. For instance, a student carrying out a marketing project might be supervised by a member of staff from the finance team. Experience has now shown that at undergraduate level this need not necessarily pose a problem. It would clearly be nonsense to assume that one could supervise projects by managing the process alone when student and supervisor interests crossed discipline boundaries (eg, management and psychology).

However, there may well be distinct advantages in managing the process rather than the content within the constraints of broad subject boundaries. Questions often asked in literature concerning research supervision at all levels are, 'How far do we provide expert support for students and how far do we encourage autonomy?' and 'At what point is ownership of the research in danger of transferring from student to supervisor?' The Winfield report (1987) stresses that 'a balance needs to be maintained between the two-fold objectives of support and autonomy'. If students receive too much support with content their independence may be impaired, but although a balance of support and autonomy is obviously needed, there is often a struggle between the desire for autonomy and the requirements of authority, resulting in tension between freedom and constraint.

Although the 1994/95 students in Sunderland Business School were matched with their supervisors on the basis of discipline expertise in order to manage both process and content, during the academic year 1995/96 students were matched in a largely random fashion with the primary emphasis on managing the process, with no noticeable disadvantage.

RESEARCH INTO STUDENT SUPERVISOR RELATIONSHIPS

It has already been suggested that, within certain boundaries of expertise, managing the process may be more important than managing the content of research in a supervision setting. If this view is accepted, a fundamental question needs to be addressed – what criteria need to be applied when matching students and supervisors?

During the first year of operating the new scheme it was noticed that some students were more likely to volunteer personal problems when having regular contact with their individual supervisors. Others reported feelings of incompatibility with their designated supervisors, and others again sought independently to develop relationships with alternative supervisors. Similar observations have been made at Masters and Doctoral level supervision. Literature in the field often expresses significant concerns over the number of students failing to complete dissertations in the social sciences and student dissatisfaction with supervision has often been cited as one of the causes. The supervisor/student relationship has often been cited as having a critical influence on the completion of postgraduate research. For example, Hockey (1991) says, 'The supervision process is, to state the obvious, a relationship. What kind of relationship evolves will heavily influence the outcome of the student's success or failure', and Rogers (1969) says that, 'The facilitation of significant learning rests upon certain attitudinal qualities that exist in the personal relationship between the facilitator and the learner'.

This raises the question of whether or not it is more important to match the work styles of supervisors and students (Phillips and Pugh, 1994) rather than matching in terms of subject discipline. This concept of matching styles impelled me to consider the relevant social and emotional aspects of human behaviour and development.

COGNITIVE STYLE

Research now being conducted into interpersonal dyad relationships seeks to investigate the significance of matching students and supervisors according to their cognitive style. Much of the work on cognitive style derives from C Jung's (1923) personality theory and the Myers–Briggs Type Indicator (MBTI), in particular, derives from these early theories (Myers, 1962). The concept of individuals possessing different cognitive styles has been discussed for several decades and writers in the field tend to agree that not only do different cognitive styles exist, but also that they can be identified. Cognitive style dimensions have been labelled:

- Convergers and divergers (Guilford, 1956);
- Field dependence–field independence (Witkin, 1962, 1976)
- Intuitive-thinking (Myers, 1962);
- Reflectivity-impulsivity (Kagan, 1965);
- Serialists-holists (Pask and Scott, 1972);
- Adaptors and innovators (Kirton, 1976);
- Activists and reflectors (Kolb, 1976);
- Wholist-analytic (Riding and Buckle, 1990);
- Intuitivists-analysts (Allinson and Hayes, 1996).

Some leading authors now believe that the various labels devised tap into similar underlying constructs. Allinson and Hayes (1996) believe that their Cognitive Styles Index (CSI) measures a superordinate dimension of cognitive style labelled 'Intuitivist' at one extreme and 'Analyst' at the other. This measure, a 38-item questionnaire that has been demonstrated to be a psychometrically sound instrument, has been used to assist my current research.

COGNITIVE STYLE AND INTERPERSONAL RELATIONSHIPS

There is evidence to suggest that interpersonal relationships are affected by differences in individual cognitive styles. Witkin (1976) confirms this view when he states that cognitive styles refer to individual differences in how people perceive, think, solve problems, learn, *and relate to others.*

In discussing the MBTI, Lawrence (1993) points out that differences in psychological type yield differences in interests, values and problem-solving techniques, which may facilitate or handicap a working relationship between two or more people. Where two individuals interacting with one another are of similar type, there is a better chance of communicating ideas. Clashes between types often arise from the very fact that opposite types can be mutually useful because each sees an aspect of the problem which the other naturally overlooks. For instance, the Intuitive type is by nature a generator of ideas who puts faith in the possible, the Sensing type is by nature someone who likes to get things done and puts faith in the actual. When an Intuitive comes up with an exciting new idea his natural course is to present it in rough and sketchy form, trusting his listener to concentrate on the main point and ignore the missing details. The Sensing type's natural reaction is to concentrate on what is missing, decide that the idea will not work and turn it down – which often results in a wasted idea and a lot of hard feeling.

Kirton (1989) observes that high Adaptors and high Innovators do not readily combine. They often tend to irritate and hold pejorative views of each other. Kirton and McArthy (1985) showed that once the theory had been explained, peoples' estimates of colleagues' scores were in close accord with self reports (with correlations at about 0.8). Kirton (1989) further states that Innovators are generally seen by Adaptors as being abrasive and insensitive despite the former's denial of having these traits. Adaptors may also be seen pejoratively by Innovators, who feel that the more extreme Adaptors are far more likely to reject them and their ideas than collaborate with them. Allinson and Hayes (1996) have reported findings consistent with some of the findings of Kirton (1989), which suggests a correlation between Kirton's 'Innovator' and their 'Intuitivist' labels and between Kirton's 'Adaptor' and their 'Analyst' ones.

CURRENT ONGOING SITUATION

Research conducted over the past three decades into the reasons for students' failure to complete dissertations has tended to support the hypothesis that the relationship between student and supervisor plays a critical part in ensuring success.

There is general agreement in the literature that the concept of cognitive style is very real, can be measured and can affect interpersonal relationships. When considering cognitive styles in a dyad relationship, where extremes exist there are four possible combinations using Allinson and Hayes (1996) labels: *Intuitivist-Intuitivist; Intuitivist-Analyst; Analyst-Analyst*, and *Analyst-Intuitivist*. My view is that these combinations are likely to lead to differences in the development of interpersonal relationships. To test this hypothesis the cognitive styles of 120 research students and their allocated supervisors for the academic year were measured using the Allinson–Hayes (1996) Cognitive Styles Index. Tape-recorded interviews are currently being carried out to determine the students' and supervisors' perception of interpersonal relationships that developed during the supervision process.

Data are also being collected from a series of supervision meetings, but because interaction includes facial expressions, gestures, bodily attitudes, emotional signs or nonverbal acts of various kinds in addition to speech, these supervision meetings are being video recorded. This information will be subjected to both quantitative and qualitative data analysis in order to support or disprove the current hypothesis.

Acknowledgement

I would like to thank my friend and mentor in life, Harry Penna Brooks, for his meticulous attention to detail when proofreading my work.

REFERENCES

Acker, S, Hill, T and Black, E (1994) 'Thesis Supervision in the Social Sciences – Managed or Negotiated', *Higher Education*, **28**, 4, 483–98.

Allinson, C W and Hayes, J (1996) 'The Cognitive Style Index: A Measure of Intuition-Analysis for Organisational Research', *Journal of Management Studies*, **33**, 1.

Bales, R F (1951) *Interaction Process Analysis*, Addison-Wesley, Cambridge, MA.

Brown, G and Atkins, M (1988) *Effective Teaching in Higher Education*, Methuen, London.

Cottrell, D J, McCrorie, P and Perrin, F (1994) 'The Personal Tutor System: An Evaluation', *Medical Journal*, **28**, 6 544–9.

Egglestone, J and Delamont, S (1983) *Supervision of Students for Research Degrees*, BERA, Birmingham.

Guilford, J P (1956) *Fundamental Statistics in Psychology and Education*, McGraw-Hill, New York.

Hill, T, Acker, S and Black, E (1994) 'Research Students and their Supervisors in Education and Psychology', in *Postgraduate Education and Training in the Social Sciences*, R G Burgess (ed.), Jessica Kingsley, London.

Hockey, J (1991) 'The Social Science PhD – A Literature Review', *Studies in Higher Education*, **16**, 3, 319–32.

Jung, C G (1923) *Psychological Types*, Routledge & Kegan Paul, London.

Kagan, J (1965) 'Impulsive and Reflective Children: Significance of Conceptual Tempo', in *Learning and the Educational Process*, J Knumboltz (ed.), Rand McNalley, Chicago.

Katz, J and Hartnett, R T (1976) *Scholars in the Making*, Ballinger, Cambridge, MA.

Kirton, M J (1976) 'Adaptors and Innovators: A Description and Measure', *Journal of Applied Psychology*, **61**, 622–9.

Kirton, M J (1989) 'Adaptors and Innovators at Work', in *Adaptors and Innovators: Style of Creativity and Problem Solving*, M J Kirton (ed), Routledge, London.

Kirton, M J, and McArthy, R (1985) 'Person and Group Estimates of the Kirton Inventory Scores', *Psychological Reports*, **57**, 1067–70.

Kolb, D A (1976) 'Management and the Learning Process', *California Management Review*, **18**, 3, 21–31.

Lawrence, G (1993) 'People Types and Tiger Stripes', *Centre for Application of Psychological Types*, Gainsville, FL.

Messick, S (1976) 'Personality Consistencies in Cognition and Creativity', in *Individuality in Learning*, S Messick and Associates (eds), Jossey-Bass, San Francisco, CA.

Myers, I B (1962) *The Myers-Briggs Type Indicator*, Consulting Psychologists Press, Palo Alto, CA.

Pask, G and Scott, B C (1972) 'Learning Strategies and Individual Competence', *International Journal of Man–Machine Studies*, **4**, 217–53.

Phillips, E, and Pugh, D S (1994) *How to get a PhD*, Open University Press, Milton Keynes.

Riding, R J and Buckle, C F (1990) *Learning Styles and Training Performance*, Sheffield Training Agency, Sheffield.

Riding, R J (1993) 'Individual Differences in Thinking: Cognitive and Neurophysiological Perspectives', *Educational Psychology*, **13**, 3&4, 267–79.

Rogers, C (1969) *Freedom to Learn*, Merrill, Hemel Hempstead.

Rudd, E (1985) *A New Look at Postgraduate Failure*, SRHE/NFER Nelson, Guilford, Surrey.

Winfield (1987) *The Social Sciences PhD: The ESRC Enquiry on Submission Rates*, Report of the Economic and Social Research Council (ESRC).

Witkin, H A, Dyke, R B, Faterson, H F and Karp, S A (1962) *Psychological Differentiation*, Wiley, New York.

Witkin, H A (1976) 'Cognitive Style in Academic Performance and in Teacher–Student Relations', in *Individuality in Learning*, S Messick and Associates (eds) Jossey-Bass, San Francisco, CA.

Wright, J and Lodwick, R (1989) 'The Process of the PhD: A Study of the First Year of Doctoral Study, *Research Papers in Education*, **4**, 22–56.

Chapter 12

The Rise of the 'Strategic Student': How Can We Adapt to Cope?

Pauline E Kneale

INTRODUCTION

There are students in universities who take a 'strategic' approach to their studies, who devote more time to sport, leisure and cultural activities or part-time work than to their university degree. This chapter describes the results of a questionnaire carried out in old and new universities in the UK to explore this phenomenon, and it explains some of the causes and implications of the issue, and the effect it can have on student learning.

When the numbers of university entrants represented some 5% of the school cohort there was a general acceptance that to gain a place at a university was worth working for and an experience to be valued. Obtaining a 'good degree' was likely to be rewarded in the job market. Through tutorial systems, staff could and did get to know individual students very well. Discipline was always necessary to encourage the more idle, but generally there was a motivation to get involved with the subject and obtain a degree.

The early to mid 1990s saw the move to a modular degree structure in many UK universities and a major increase in numbers. There were programme revisions, increased access to a wide range of elective subjects and a move towards the publication and rationalization of university rules across institutions (Green, 1995; Thorne, 1991; Wright and Ager, 1992). With increasing class sizes, the traditional individual nature of university teaching is disappearing in all years. The link between staff and student is getting weaker and the nature of teaching and learning is radically changing. At the same time the attitudes and expectations of students coming to university are also changing. What has not changed is the manner in which universities attempt to monitor, discipline and control student academic activities. There is still a background assumption that:

(a) students want to be at university; and

(b) students are interested in the degree subject they are studying.

My view is that these two statements are less true than many colleagues think.

This paper presents the results of a pilot survey of undergraduate tutors to try to ascertain whether student demotivation and strategic choices are widespread. It thus represents a preliminary stage, the next being the intention to explore the attitudes of current students.

QUESTIONNAIRE RESPONSES

Postal questionnaires were sent to tutors in departments of Biology, Civil Engineering, English, French, Geography, Geology, History, and Philosophy in 12 old and 10 new universities. There were 52 replies, of which 43 could be used for numerical analysis. The return rate was just over 30%. Table 12.1 summarizes the numbers of departments that acknowledged some degree of strategic behaviour among their students.

	Departments									
	English	History	Geo-graphy	Engin-eering	Biology	Lang-uages	Philos-ophy	Geology	Others	Total %
Strategic behaviour reported	2	1	6	2	5	1	0	1	3	41
No evidence of strategic behaviour	3	4	7	3	0	4	2	3	4	59
Total	5	5	13	5	5	5	2	4	7	100

Table 12.1 *Incidence of strategic behaviour by subject area*

There were two additional positive responses, both from old universities, which acknowledged there were demotivated students but the department was not identified. Four 'nil' responses were returned from departments not initially targeted, one each from Law, Medicine, Architecture and a faculty of Arts and Education. A very firm 'yes, we have a major problem' came from a Computer Studies department. Three respondents were not prepared to answer the questionnaire offering among their reasoning:

'Yes, we have seen some (students of this type) but are in no way prepared to answer such a questionnaire.'

'Not prepared to respond with anecdotal information that might misrepresent the positions of students with real problems.'

'Students of the type you describe have never been members of this department and I doubt whether any such student has attended this university.'

It was recognized from the start that this questionnaire needed to be answered by undergraduate tutors or who had experience of handling student matters over a number of years. More than 80% of the replies that came from heads of department fell into the 'No problem here' category, and include the respondents not prepared to complete the questionnaire. At the other end of the scale some undergraduate tutors provided pages of additional notes. A number of tutors commented that research-based heads of department were unlikely to realize this type of student behaviour exists, typically: 'Successive heads of department are just not interested in problem students – this is left to year tutors to sort out with the (university) administration.'

Table 12.1 suggests that there is a situation, albeit small, that needs to be discussed. Given the small numbers it is impossible to generalize about departmental differences, but there was sympathy from respondents to the view that strategic behaviour is more common in departments that follow from mainstream 'A' levels, such as biology and geography, and less evident in departments where a candidate makes a change in academic direction, for example to geology or philosophy. It is easier to follow a subject you are familiar with without really thinking about your course choices.

The questionnaire asked respondents to indicate whether they had in the last ten years encountered students expressing these kinds of statements. Where the answer is 'Yes' the percentage and total numbers of students involved are indicated in Table 12.2.

Happily the majority of respondents are not seeing seriously defaulting students. However, it is notable that the majority of the 'yes' answers come from departments in the old university sector. It is possible that this kind of student has been more common in the old polytechnic sector and systems have evolved to handle them.

Respondents were then asked if they could give other examples of student statements of this type. The abbreviated list includes:

'I only came 'cos it will help me get a better job.'

'I am only doing this degree to get a job.'

'It is what is expected of me.'

'My family insisted that I study for a profession/job, not the arts/social science degree I wished to do.'

'My father insisted I do this degree.'

'I applied to seaside universities so I can surf.'

'...for the night life, I wanted a course in a happening city.'

'I don't need to pass this module, I'll pass (the year) anyway.'

'I can pass the year without doing the course work, so stop hassling me to give it in.'

Questions and answers posited in our survey. Respondents were asked if they encountered students who were likely to demonstrate these kinds of attitudes.	Respondents who agreed (number) % (no. of students encountered)	Respondents who disagreed (number) %
Q. Presumably since you chose to study X you are interested in some parts of the subject? **A.** *No.*	(8) 19 (1-10)	(35) 81
Q. You chose to come to university to do X. **A.** *No I didn't, I don't want to be at university, I want to be at work, but there are no work alternatives where I live.*	(5) 13 (1-3+)	(38) 87
Q. Why are you doing a degree at all? **A.** *Because that's what you do after school, isn't it?*	(13) 30 (1-15, av. 4.4)	(30) 70
Q. Why are you doing this subject in the first place? **A** *That's what I found easiest at school, but I'm not really bothered about whether I do X or Y, I don't really care.*	(9) 21 (2-numerous)	(34) 79
Q. Why did you fill out the UCAS form? **A.** *Didn't, our sixth form tutor handed round the UCCA/UCAS forms and we all kind of filled them in.*	(2) 5 (1-3)	(41) 95
Q. Why did you choose the University of X? **A.** *No reason, just put down six places at random, mostly we used football teams.*	(4) 10 (2-20)	(39) 90
Q. Did you look at a prospectus for each university you chose? **A.** *I never looked at a prospectus.*	(9) 21 (1-10)	(34) 79

Table 12.2 *Questions and answers*

'I do not read books.'

'I have a right to a grant, it's not a privilege, and it's up to me how much work I do, not anyone else.'

Reading, Leeds, Birmingham and Manchester are quoted as universities chosen 'so I could go to the football'.

A number of tutors who fall into the 'no' category for the specific questions above commented:

'We have poorly motivated students but not in the extreme category as the ones you are thinking of.'

'I think this is becoming a more common phenomena each year, but not as blatant as your questions indicate.'

'This description fits about 40–80% of the students I teach, and their lack of interest is quite amazing, as is the lack of initiative. On the one hand, it does little for the lecturers' morale and there is little room for a two-way relationship between staff and students. However, my students are less overt in their complacency than the characters your questionnaire describes. No student has formally admitted to me that this is how he or she feels, consequently I cannot answer your questionnaire. Nevertheless, we have a major problem… Moreover, I expect the situation to get worse rather than better.'

'Cases are not as extreme as suggested here. Basically these students end up with an inferior, poor degree.'

Tutors estimates of the proportion of students acting in a strategic manner ranged from 'none' to 'most of the class'.

Over 40% of the respondents indicated that they are seeing students for whom the nature of the degree and degree work has a lower priority in the week than members of the teaching staff would wish, typically:

'We do not have students who don't want to be here in the first place, but we have to deal with many who disappoint their tutors by seeing their degree as a necessary stage in their career path to a well-paid job rather than as a passionate academic interest. The tutors most disappointed are those older staff who regret the days when they were able to teach potential scholars rather than potential financial advisors.'

Evidence offered for the existence of the 'strategic student' includes:

- refusal to contribute in classes for which there is no mark;
- popularity of modules without examinations;
- lack of attendance at modules where assessment is essay based;
- late submission despite penalties;
- attendance at modules up to the point where topics chosen for assessment are covered;

- non-attendance at exams where continual assessment has already ensured a pass;
- non-submission of continually assessed work after the minimum pass grade is achieved;
- decisions to entirely ignore 10 or 20 credit modules that can be failed without compromising the final degree result;
- students prepared to explain that this is what they are doing.

As an academic body we can amend module rules to state that completion of all practicals in a module is required and take class registers, but with large classes this is time consuming, open to fraud and irritates students who should be treated as responsible adults. Generally by second and third year most of these 'strategic students' have got involved, are performing, and most get 2:2 degrees. The real problem comes in level 1 classes where there is limited incentive to perform well. If it is only required that level 1 is passed, with degree classification dependent solely on performance in years 2 and 3, there is little incentive to do more than the minimum at level 1.

Asked to comment on the impact of such students at departmental level, responses fall into four general categories.

1. *Elective issues*
Responses in this category included:

> 'As part of modularization many students are required to take modules from other degree programmes, on the grounds of broadening their studies. This is where I see problems becoming more acute.'

> 'Because of our very high entry grades, AAB, we don't have a problem with single honours students. However, students from other departments, and ours working in other departments, are prone to the "why bother?" attitude, and our marking systems allow them to carry on even if in many cases they fail.'

2. *Staff time issues*
Responses included:

> 'They cause a great deal of administrative time, trouble and effort; the 4–5 students in this first year took up days of my time, sorting out, form filling...'

> 'Had one who wasted hours of staff time, chasing up and reporting unsatisfactory work and attendance. At the end of the day there was nothing we could do.'

> 'We spend a ridiculous amount of time and effort chasing up poorly motivated students with little effect. We would rather spend it encouraging good students.'

3. Assessment issues

Responses received included:

> 'It may interest you to know that this term I have observed a sharp increase in students who don't care if their essays are late despite penalties of two marks per day. Also, an increase in the number of students who we are talking about, don't turn up, don't care and seem impervious to rebuke or penalty.'

> 'Student observation of colleagues graduating despite failures in one to four or more modules reinforces the "why bother?" attitude.'

> 'Frankly, failing a student is in some cases fair to the other students who feel that their own performances are devalued by students who pass having done the minimum of work.'

> 'Other students understandably feel resentful of the strategic student who still gets a 2:2; we can usually persuade them that the quality of the education they experience is more important than the acquisition of a qualification. However, I think that while you can use this argument with pleasant, polite students and they will then leave your office, they do not really believe you and it ignores the issue.'

4. Changing student attitudes

In this category, responses included:

> 'The strategic student has always existed. In less paternalistic regimes, and ones less hunted by TQA, they were able to keep a low profile. In the current climate when we are conscious of our need to please the clients, they have a higher nuisance value, but I cannot believe that they are numerous enough to constitute a serious problem. What has changed is the willingness of students to pretend to an interest that they do not feel and, with the decline in status of academic study, students feel more aggressive in response to questions such as those listed.'

> 'We need to be able to feel we set the highest academic standards, but both staff and students must recognize that there is scope for students to work with less than total commitment and still get a degree.'

Departments without strategic students

Departments where students of this type are not seen as a problem include those where modularization was not linked to a change in the classification rules for degrees. Evidence from the questionnaire returns suggests that where the penalties for module failure are very severe the strategic student is less apt to emerge. A department where failure of one module reduces the final degree awarded by a class, and two modules means failure of the entire degree, reports no evidence of strategic behaviour. From another:

> 'We count all courses in degree assessment so that students cannot afford to ignore any module, although it may happen very occasionally in years 1 and 2 where a resit is available. Problem students of your extreme sort are not

seen; by final year our least committed members are usually cheerfully involved. Students calculating the "minimum necessary" rarely persist into final year.'

Organizers of programmes with little or no module choice commented that the whole class group is cohesive and committed.

Gender issues

I thought that there might be a gender aspect to this phenomenon (Ingleton, 1995), as I have encountered more men prepared to admit having a strategy to 'throw' modules. Comments were wide ranging:

'Definitely a more male activity, maybe one women in 16 years, very rare.'

'Girls like this do exist, but are usually more amenable to being steered back onto the academic path.'

'I think this is equally a male and female phenomenon, but girls are less blatant about it, happier to appear to conform.'

'Although their style may differ the attitude is equally true of both sexes. Girls are just quieter about it, and are often given greater tolerance because it is assumed to be more characteristic of the lads.'

It appears that the women are less likely to be obvious about their strategies and take the 'safer' options, missing parts of modules, rather than blatantly failing one or two. At the other end of the scale, some of our best mature students are strategically juggling home, family and study commitments to maximize their opportunities.

DISCUSSION

From the start modularization aimed to maximize flexibility, to encourage education to suit the needs of the continuously diversifying workforce (Marshall and Tucker, 1992), and to encourage students to identify their personal academic needs in relation to their potential job ambitions. The degree certificate should make clear to employers what they have achieved. (Scottish Education Department, 1984; Theodossin, 1986). The responses suggest there are few problems with mature students, those returning to education with knowledge of the changing demands of the workplace. Where workplace education is available, there is evidence of significant demand for further educational opportunities (*Times Educational Supplement*, 1990).

Electives

One of our respondents commented:

'Electives are counter-productive, offering choice to those ill-equipped to choose. By saying that students can pick any additional 20–40 credits, do we devalue them? If we cannot be bothered to fix up an integrated programme, why should they value their random programme, often at first year chosen in a haze and stampede at initial registration? The frustration of long queues...'

The elective system is being used well and imaginatively by many students. What may be needed is for the elective elements of degrees, especially at level 1, to be more supported and valued by staff. For the less motivated student, the choice is very confusing. Many students choose degree courses without noticing the elective component involved. The confusion of university arrival and registration includes a commitment to electives that commonly make up a third of the first year. Information is available in handbooks but the students' attention is focused on main subject matters. The choice of modules is frequently rushed, comments such as 'I wanted to do X, but there was a long queue at the desk so I signed up for Y' are not unusual. Not surprisingly, such students are less committed to their electives. It might help if we could:

- get much more information about electives to students prior to arrival at university and the scrum of registration.
- show the student that staff value the role of electives by insisting a pass is required for progression.

Staff time

The time involved in chasing up defaulters, especially from other departments, and the waste of time when it involves students choosing to fail, was clearly a source of much staff frustration. There is some support for suggesting a heavy hand with defaulters in the first semester. It might help if:

- it is made clear that it is the student's responsibility to attend and perform – students are over 18, if they choose to miss a class, that's their problem;
- we could take the onus off tutors to police performance;
- we reviewed methods for tracking and reporting unsatisfactory progress at university level to allow for this facet of student behaviour.

Assessment issues

Student behaviour is assessment led (Entwistle, 1987; Boud, 1995). This is seen within modules when non-marked components are ignored, and at programme level where modules may be failed. While it may irritate the tutor, the strategic student is optimizing time and effort, concentrating on module elements for which there are rewards. The best students are using the time released for sport, drama and other activities, maximizing their university experience and opportunities. The consequence of this well-used freedom is similar behaviour from less committed students where the time released is used less actively. That is the individual's choice. If the rules allow failure then we must expect it to happen.

I think this is an unanticipated consequence of modularization. In allowing students to fail 10–20 credits we teach them to 'play the system', to balance work and other activities. For some employers, this exactly the right training for employment. In the long term, evidence of module failure in transcripts of module grades achieved may not help a student's or a university's image (Parlour, 1996).

Within modules, continual assessment, such as the assessed test at the end of week 2, forces students to interact with the material immediately, which is motivating. Many replies commented that the key was involvement with appropriate rewards. There were a number of respondents who commented that failure and expulsion were almost impossible, given university procedures. With the expansion in intake, it must be expected that there will be more failures. The following statements cover the main comments:

'It should be easier to suspend a student.'

'The very rare expulsion has sent salutary ripples round the department.'

'They should be free to fail – and more courage should be shown in facing up to that by staff. We are almost too tolerant for fear we will be seen as bad teachers.'

'Use of the ordinary degree, demotion at the end of year 2 for poor performers, make the honours degree worth getting.'

'Fail and remove students after two warnings. Stop feeling guilty about them, as if we are betraying some code of misguided decency. In tolerating what is often dumb insolence, a contempt for the system, we are visibly letting down the other "working" students, and they know it.'

We need to examine procedures for progression and failure.

Changing student attitudes

'Motivation is a major issue here, and is maybe increasingly problematic. We have problems with students who are basically here to get a degree for employment purposes and are not necessarily interested in the subject matter.'

Students know that a university degree is not necessarily a passport to employment. The practicalities of finance mean that many students have to take part-time jobs and this inevitably takes away some of the feelings of satisfaction with university life. It reduces study time and leads to non-attendance where academic and work commitments clash. Survey responses acknowledge increasing problems of attendance in classes after 4pm and in the 12–2.15pm slots. There are few practical suggestions about combating this phenomenon, beyond recognizing that this is a fact of modern academic life and trying to allow for it.

Permitting students to sign up for classes rather than assigning them to slots allows the student to optimize university and work commitments. Staff should be sympathetic to difficulties of tutorial classes after 4pm. An engineering colleague reported problems of non-attendance in practicals where students are assigned particular teams and laboratory times. Asking students to indicate their work commitments and then setting up teams and times that did not conflict with outside jobs revealed 70% of the class with jobs, three exceeding 20 hours a week. Timetabling to maximize attendance is likely to increase motivation, since it shows an appreciation of the facts of student life, and makes teaching more effective. When the options are to attend a lecture or to earn the cash for food and rent, most people will choose to earn the money.

CONCLUSIONS

There is a cognitive disjunction between our expectation of students, and the actuality. We expect them to do well, be committed and enthusiastic about their subject, but we value what they do so little that under some modular systems they can fail 40+ credits and graduate with honours. The 'strategic' student who chooses to fail some modules is simply at one end of a spectrum which has at the top end the extremely bright and committed student who makes some particular arrangements to facilitate learning. At the less motivated end of the spectrum, students are less easy or rewarding to manage. Monitoring their progress can be extremely time consuming and ultimately pointless under present procedures.

Problems with strategic students are acknowledged in 41% of the departments that responded, the majority in the old university sector. The evidence suggests we are seeing an increase in students who arrive without having made a positive choice in their university or degree topic, selecting universities without consulting the prospectus, in 'towns with good football teams' or 'seaside universities where you can surf', students who 'came to university because that is what you do next', not as a really thought-out choice. These students have high-quality 'A' levels, they are bright and perfectly capable if motivated of getting a 2:1 degree, but profess to having no particular interest in higher education. They take a strategic approach to the problem, read the rules, know what is compulsory, and what can be ignored. Their numbers are small, but with large classes and in student-centred sessions, they have a demotivating impact on their colleagues.

Staff should recognize that following expansion of the university system many students are not primarily academic. It is unrealistic to expect all students to be fully committed to all modules.

Following all the changes at modularization it is appropriate to examine the impacts it made. This survey of undergraduate tutors suggests there are issues to be addressed at university level relating to electives, assessment and monitoring and management of progress.

REFERENCES

Boud, D (1995) 'Assessment and Learning: Contradictory or Complementary?' in *Assessment for Learning in Higher Education*, P Knight (ed.), Kogan Page, London, pp.35–48.

Entwistle, N (1987) 'A Model of the Teaching and Learning Process', in *Student Learning: Research in Education and Cognitive Psychology*, J T E Richardson, M W Eysenck and D W Piper (eds), SHRE, pp.13–28

Green, M F (1995) 'Transforming British Higher Education: A View from Across the Atlantic', *Higher Education*, **29**, 225–39

Ingleton, C (1995) 'Gender and Learning: Does Emotion Make a Difference?' *Higher Education*, **30**, 323–35

Marshall, R and Tucker, M (1992) *Thinking for a Living: Education and the Wealth of Nations*, Basic Books, New York.

Parlour, J W (1996) 'A Critical Analysis of Degree Classification Procedures and Outcomes', *Higher Education Review*, **28**, 2, 25–39

Scottish Education Department (SED)(1984) *Guide for Parents and Children*, SED, Edinburgh.

Theodossin, E (1986) *The Modular Market*, Further Education Staff College, Bristol.

Thorne, CR (1991) 'Modularisation and Geography: A JGHE Arena Symposium', *Journal of Geography in Higher Education*, **15**, 2, 177–20.

Times Educational Supplement (1990) 'Agreement between Ford and its Trade Unions', 31 August.

Wright, S and Ager, D (1992) 'Considerations of Democratization and Elitism in Higher Education in the United Kingdom', *Higher Education in Europe*, **17**, 4, 24–33.

Chapter 13

From Teacher to Facilitator of Collaborative Enquiry

Lorraine Stefani and David Nicol

INTRODUCTION

Pressures for change

Over the past decade the higher education sector has been subject to unprecedented pressures to change its character and role. Some of these pressures have affected university governance, organization and finance (Wagner, 1995), while others have had a more direct impact on staff and students – modularization, semesterization, a blurring of the boundaries between further and higher education, a massive increase in student numbers and an increasingly diverse student population. The very purpose of the university is being challenged. High-level specialist knowledge and understanding of a subject are no longer regarded as sufficient qualifications for graduates entering the rapidly changing economic and employment base. Employers are increasing the premium on graduates who can show evidence of creativity, independence and initiative, combined with a sense of flexibility and adaptability. New opportunities for innovative courses are unfolding as a result of the information technology revolution, which has enabled concepts and information to be manipulated and communicated in new ways. A combination of scientific discoveries and new technology are also leading to the blurring of subject boundaries and to the emergence of new disciplines.

Not surprisingly, in the face of such a rapid and dramatic change within the culture of higher education, tensions and dysfunctions between the old and new have appeared. Some university staff seem to be trying to hang on to the vestiges of a traditional and elitist system of education and appear reluctant to acknowledge fully the extent to which the external changes require them to devise new teaching and learning approaches more appropriate to a mass higher education system.

Students are also more aware now than in the past of their entitlement to good teaching. They are no longer blind to the fact that some of their teachers are more interested in producing good research than in improving their teaching abilities, because research determines academic reputations. Pedagogy has been neglected in many universities until now, partly because being recognized as a good teacher has had little effect on lecturers' career prospects. Indeed, until recently, in the traditional university the responsibility for failure in learning has been attributed to deficiencies in the individual student and there has been little attempt to relate poor learning to poor standards of teaching (Ainley, 1994).

The current upheavals in higher education bring into sharper relief not only the challenges facing students entering higher education but also the challenges facing teachers and tutors to develop a pedagogy for the new higher education: a pedagogy based on an understanding of the impediments to student learning in higher education and on an understanding of what teachers can do to help students to learn. This chapter focuses on one aspect of that pedagogy – sharing students' and tutors' conceptions of some of the key aspects of the higher education context. It raises some important issues that the new pedagogy will have to consider and it describes some ways of addressing these. Research on learning and teaching provides the evidence upon which the paper is based, but critical aspects of the paper also derive from experience gained during consultation with departments. These consultations were collaborative action research projects with teaching staff in their own departments aimed at improving some aspect of teaching or learning identified by members of the department.

SHARING CONCEPTIONS OF TEACHING AND LEARNING

The learning environment and students' conceptions

Educational consultants who are invited into a new subject department inhabit a rather strange role. In one sense they are teachers tasked with providing educational knowledge and advice to higher education teachers about learning and instruction. On the other hand, they are learners who must come to grips with a new disciplinary domain, a specialist territory. Although armed with knowledge of the factors that are essential to the development of an effective teaching and learning environment, the consultant often has little knowledge of the subject discipline or the disciplinary culture. Yet the role of the consultant is to contextualize and adapt his or her expertise to that discipline and culture.

In many ways the situation facing the consultant mirrors that of students entering a discipline for the first time, except that students, unlike consultants, have even less knowledge of the culture of higher education.

Students must learn to function in a quite unfamiliar environment, they must learn what is valued within that environment, what behaviours are acceptable and unacceptable and the rules of engagement especially with staff. New students must be inducted into a disciplinary community and must internalize the framework of rules that the community abides by (Becher, 1989). This framework is defined through a variety of formal and informal processes such as the structure and content of courses, the learning methods used, the intellectual skills to be acquired and the applications of the disciplinary subject content. But students often have difficulty deciphering the requirements of the discipline because the transmission of subject-specific academic information is deeply embedded within the overall communication of the norms of the cultural community.

Research on student learning supports the contention that the physical and social environment have an important bearing on how students learn. A basic distinction in the current higher education literature is between students who adopt a deep learning approach and those who adopt a surface learning approach (Ramsden, 1992). Deep learning is obviously valued over surface learning in higher education. Yet whether students adopt a surface or deep approach appears to depend on students' intentions, which in turn depend on how students conceive the learning environment and the formal and informal requirements of task and assessment demands.

It is easy for teachers whose work-related communication occurs within a cultural context to overlook the difficulty that new students experience when first exposed to an unfamiliar field of study. But consultants entering a new department are constantly reminded of this difficulty both in terms of their own experience and through students' comments. It is, for example, quite common for students to report that the relevance of the subject did not make sense to them until the second or third year of their studies. It is therefore important that staff in individual departments consider how students are initiated into and come to terms with the culture of the discipline.

When this issue has formed part of the consultancy discussions with staff and students in departments, staff have often decided to organize sessions with the students with the aim of finding out what the latters' preconceptions are regarding the discipline. What has emerged in these discussions are clear mismatches between the expectations of tutors and students' understandings of these expectations.

Forms of representation and students' conceptions

In addition to the social and physical environment, it is equally important to address other issues relating more specifically to the culture of learning within the discipline. A second area of concern is therefore the types of representation and symbol systems that students are expected to learn to use to convey subject knowledge. Forms of representation are different in different disciplines: for example, essays in history, drawings and models in architecture, case study reports in marketing and posters and scientific papers in science subject areas. It is often assumed that students enter higher education knowing how to present their work in these symbolic, iconic and practical forms, but experience during consultancy suggests that the situation is more complex than one might first think. For instance, in many disciplines, the favoured means of representation is the essay. Yet it is clear that students have conceptual difficulties in understanding what an essay is, how it is to be used to represent disciplinary thinking, or how it is produced by competent scholars.

These difficulties are not surprising given that students are rarely exposed to the cognitive processes that good essay writers engage in. These processes are normally internal to the writer and are therefore hidden from students. But the research on essay writing shows that students must develop appropriate conceptualizations of essays and essay writing processes if they are to develop good writing strategies. Bereiter and Scardamalia (1987) have shown that inappropriate conceptions about essays and the writing processes are a major cause of poor essay production by students. In a similar vein, Hounsell (1987) and Norton (1990) have shown that the nature of students' conceptions about what an essay is (eg, an argument supported by evidence or an arrangement of facts) actually determines students' essay writing strategies. In fact, the greater the divergence between students' and tutors' conceptions of essays, the poorer the performance of students in terms of marks awarded

Teaching methods and students' conceptions

The different teaching methods commonly used in higher education exist because they help develop in students different kinds of skills and learning strategies. But interviews with students about methods reveal a variety of areas of conceptual confusion about what the objectives of these methods are, what skills should be acquired during participation in the methods and about how they are expected to interact.

For example, we have discovered in discussions with new students that they have quite vague conceptions about what a tutorial is or what it means to engage in tutorial discussion. Once again the literature is quite consistent with the findings of these discussions. For example, Tiberius (1990) writing about tutorials and seminars, notes the failure of tutors to convey to students what behaviours are expected in tutorials and what kinds of learning are expected.

During interviews with students participating in practical classes in some science subjects, we found that many believed that these classes involved little more than carrying out a set of routine procedures, following a recipe, the product of which elicits little excitement. Although the stated purpose of practical classes is to enhance student learning and skills development and to enable students to apply theoretical concepts to practical problems, this is often poorly understood by students.

The implications of these findings about methods is that tutors must look for ways of sharing their conceptions with students about the implicit rules governing interaction in different teaching and learning contexts, and to apprise them of the purposes and skills to be acquired from settings such as tutorials and practicals.

A WAY FORWARD – USING CLASSROOM EVALUATION TECHNIQUES

This chapter has so far focused on the problems that new students face in three key aspects of the learning culture of higher education: developing appropriate conceptions about teaching methods, disciplinary modes of representation and environmental contexts that are conducive to their learning. To be effective, students' conceptions should be more closely matched to those of their tutors. However, conceptions of complex processes don't occur instantly, they are developed over time. One way that this could be facilitated is to provide repeated opportunities for tutor–student dialogue during learning. Unfortunately, as a result of the move towards mass higher education outlined in the introduction, tutor–student dialogue around teaching and learning has been greatly reduced.

What should dialogue achieve?

Dialogue is necessary for a number of reasons. It is necessary as a means of externalizing both students' and tutors' thinking processes. This would allow tutors and students to share their understandings of teaching and assessment methods and modes of representation. It would also allow students to make comparisons between their thinking and that of their tutors and would allow them to make adjustments and changes in their study methods that would improve their learning. Establishing an ethos of dialogue can offer a powerful means of providing feedback on both the teaching and learning processes. It is, however, essential that any new teaching method does not place an inordinate burden on teaching staff.

How can dialogue be reintroduced?

The authors of this chapter have been exploring one low-tech procedure that offers a way of reintroducing dialogue into the teaching–learning environment. It is based on a modification of the Classroom Assessment Technique originally promoted by Angelo and Cross (1993). After describing the technique we discuss how it might help to address some of the issues raised in the earlier part of this chapter.

Description of technique

An example of the technique as originally proposed by Angelo and Cross is the 'one-minute-paper'. Five minutes before the end of a lecture the lecturer puts two questions on the overhead projector to which the students are expected to respond in writing on an index card or a half sheet of paper. In this example, the questions are typically variants of the following.

- What was the main point of today's lecture?
- What questions remain outstanding for you?

Students' responses only comprise two or three sentences per question and they are handed in anonymously (they don't put their names on the cards) on the way out of the class. Students are normally shown the two questions before the lecture begins and told that it will end five minutes early in order to address the questions.

An important aspect of this technique is the opportunity it provides for giving students rapid feedback on their learning. This is achieved by limiting the time taken to categorize responses. The lecturer normally reads through and sorts the responses to the questions into two or three categories (eg, good and poor) to obtain a snapshot of the class understanding. The next step is for the tutor to feed back his or her evaluation of the quality of the responses to students. This is normally implemented at the next meeting with the same group of students.

This step is essential to close the feedback loop. The tutor might replay one or two 'good' and a few 'poor' responses on the overhead and indicate whether the majority of students have understood or misunderstood newly presented concepts. Where there are difficulties the tutor might spend some time clarifying these. An important role for the tutor here is to inform students about what she or he intends to do in the future in order to facilitate students' understanding. For example, if students are interpreting asides given in the lecture as the main point the tutor might signal that she or he intends to provide a summary of the main points. The tutor would in the same context also suggest changes that students might make to improve their learning. In the lecture example, the tutor may have noticed that students are trying to write down everything said and suggest that students listen for longer and try to record only the main ideas and linkages and fill in more detail after the lecture. This advice introduces instruction about learning strategies into the discourse. In the authors' experience in using this technique and supporting staff in using it for the first time it will take 1–2 minutes to process each response, the timing decreasing with practice.

This technique can be used in almost any teaching situation and is particularly suited to large classes where anonymity of reponses is assured. As with other innovations success depends on being informed in advance about the purpose and nature of the procedure.

ADVANTAGES OF USING THE CLASSROOM EVALUATION TECHNIQUE

Although this technique appears to be rather simple it can serve as a means of creating powerful tutor–student dialogue. The one-minute paper focuses on course-related knowledge and skills. However, the technique can also be used to create dialogue around students' understandings about the learning environment, forms of representation and about learners' reactions to instruction (see below).

Classroom evaluation is dialogical in that it involves the externalization of students' thinking through writing and the sharing of conceptions. Tutors can formulate questions that target areas of students' thinking that are important to learning but are not normally accessible in classroom settings. By replaying students' responses together with the tutors' interpretation of these responses (and sometimes examples of tutors' responses to the same questions) students are able to compare their own conceptions with those of their tutors (and other students). The advice offered by tutors during the replay can help students devise strategies to close the gap between student and tutor conceptions.

The technique not only allows tutors to evaluate students' thinking within the learning context, it also allows teachers to elicit feedback on the effectiveness of their teaching approach. So it benefits the teacher as well as the student. Importantly, this technique gives a clear signal that tutors are interested in students' learning.

Although it does take time to administer the classroom evaluation, the advantages far outweigh the marginal loss in teaching time. The technique is a continuous process which is easy to integrate. It gives teachers a way of finding out about areas of confusion in students' thinking and it provides an early warning about student problems. While the technique could be used in every class, this would probably be counter-productive unless the questions were quite varied. Experience suggests that if a tutor has a block of teaching the procedure might be used once a week or at an early stage or part way through the block and again near the end of the block.

ADAPTING THE USE OF THE CLASSROOM EVALUATION TECHNIQUE

The technique of classroom evaluation can be manipulated to create dialogue around key issues associated with the culture of learning in higher education such as those highlighted above. Described briefly below are examples of how the technique could be used to share conceptions of the disciplinary learning environment, forms of representation and methods of teaching. It is beyond the scope of this chapter to discuss specific outcomes of the examples quoted below, but they are included as illustrations of adapting the technique to different situations. Further research into the impact on student learning of using the classroom evaluation technique is currently underway and preliminary data indicates a very positive response from both staff and students.

TEACHING AND LEARNING ENVIRONMENT

Within a disciplinary induction session for students who had only attended classes over a period of three weeks, students were posed the following question in the form of a classroom evaluation.

Conceptions
How do your previous learning experiences differ from the learning you think is expected of you in this higher education institution? Give the example that has most affected you.

Feedback
The tutors may recognize responses that imply different routes into higher education and sort the responses according to the expressions of different experiences. To replay a selection of these replies might well serve to enhance students' understanding of each other.

Action
The evaluation and replay should be followed by an interactive discussion session focusing firstly on commonalities of experience and dialogue around adapting and compromising teaching and learning methods, taking both staff and student limitations into consideration.

FORMS OF REPRESENTATION

Conceptions
Within a discipline that favours essay writing as a means of representation of knowledge, a strategy for sharing conceptions could include provision of a handbook description of essays and timetabled discussion sessions on essay writing encompassed by the classroom evaluation questions:

• What in your opinion are the essential characteristics of a good essay?

• What processes are necessary to construct a good essay?

Feedback

The tutors' role in this case is to categorize the responses into 'good' and 'poor', replay some of the replies and highlight areas for discussion.

Action

Help to clear up students misconceptions by showing the tutor response to the questions. Provide students with short writing tasks to build up writing skills and provide examplars of good and bad essays to illustrate some of the important points of essays and essay writing. Repeat the classroom evaluation at a later stage in the course. This is an ideal strategy for first-year classes and can help to build students' confidence at an early stage in an undergraduate course.

TEACHING METHODS

Conceptions

It is remarkably common to hear tutors complain about students' lack of participation in tutorials, and it is also common to hear students indicate that they don't really know what is expected of them in a tutorial. Students in the early years of study can be very shy about making verbal responses in what might feel to them like a very exposed situation. For this reason the classroom evaluation technique can provide a powerful tool to initiate dialogue. In a tutorial at an early stage of a course, after welcoming the students and ensuring introductions are made, the tutor could share his or her ideas about the programme of tutorials, allowing for interaction. To put students at their ease it is a good idea to set evaluation questions such as:

• What do you think is expected of you in the tutorial setting?
• What do you think is the role of the tutor in a tutorial setting?

Feedback

With good management it may be possible to categorize the responses very quickly in the same tutorial period by giving the students a short task or simply by suggesting they use the next few minutes chatting to each other. The tutor can then replay a selection of responses including their own response.

Action

A very effective use of this classroom evaluation is to suggest that the students discuss in small groups a set of groundrules for tutorials based on agreements reached with respect to tutor and student conceptions.

DISCUSSION

We have sought to highlight some of the key areas of the learning culture of higher education which can pose as blocks to the facilitation of active learning in a constantly changing environment if common conceptions of expectations are not shared by students and teachers or tutors. The challenge for teaching staff in higher education is to create a culture of dialogue in which staff and students merge their ideas to create a community of scholars. A simple strategy for initiating dialogue which can be manipulated to suit a variety of situations, has been presented. This strategy enables staff and students to reach a common understanding of the learning environment, the types of learning deemed appropriate and the roles and responsibilities of both staff and students to create a mass higher education system suited to the needs of a changing society.

REFERENCES

Ainley, P (1994) *Degrees Of Difference: Higher Education in the 1990s,* Lawrence and Wishart.

Angelo, T A and Cross, K P (1993) *Classroom Assessment Techniques,* Jossey-Bass, San Francisco, CA.

Becher, T (1989) *Academic Tribes and Territories,* The Society for Research into Higher Education (SRHE) and Open University Press, Buckingham.

Bereiter, C and Scardamalia, M (1987) *The Psychology of Written Composition,* Lawrence Erlbaum Associates, Hillsdale, NJ.

Hounsell, D A (1987) 'Learning and Essay Writing', in *The Experience of Learning,* F Marton, D Hounsel and N Entwistle (eds), Scottish Academic Press, Edinburgh.

Norton, L S (1990) 'Essay Writing: What Really Counts?' *Higher Education,* **20,** 411–42.

Ramsden, P (1992) *Learning to Teach in Higher Education,* Routledge, London.

Sadler, D R (1983) 'Evaluation and the Improvement of Academic Learning', *Journal of Higher Education,* **54,** 60–69.

Tiberius, R G (1990) *Small Group Teaching: A Trouble-shooting Guide,* Monograph Series 22, The Ontario Institute for Studies in Education, OISE Press, Ontario.

Wagner, L (1995) 'A Thirty Year Perspective: From the Sixties to the Nineties', in *The Changing University,* T Schuller (ed.), SRHE and Open University Press, Buckingham.

Chapter 14

Issues of Power and Control: Moving from 'Expert' to 'Facilitator'

Pete Sayers and Bob Matthew

INTRODUCTION

In theory university lecturers should have less trouble with issues of power and control than other teachers. School teachers act *in loco parentis* and are required to control the behaviour of school students, many of whom are not at school voluntarily. The vast majority of university students, on the other hand, are there by choice and their behaviour can be assumed to be that of responsible adults. Lecturers should be able to operate in less controlling ways than school teachers. In reality, however, most of the teaching techniques used by university lecturers are still very controlling.

It is clear from our experience that many lecturers would like to change this situation to one where the students themselves take control of their own learning. The problems that are yet to be solved are: how can this be done, and how can it be done *effectively* while working within a large, highly structured institution such as a university?

The terms 'power' and 'control' need defining, and we shall attempt a working definition below – not one drawn from much of the literature on the subject (to do that properly would take up too much of our space here), but one that will enable us to relate notions of power and control to one specific theoretical model, the application of which to university teaching is the main discussion point of this chapter. We shall define power in terms of 'role power' and 'personal power' and look at the way our working use of those terms has derived from the world of counselling and therapy; and we shall explore what we term the 'control paradox'. We shall also explain how we see the issues of power and control relating to the contrasting roles for academics of 'expert' or 'facilitator'.

The theoretical framework we use is Blanchard's 'Situational Leadership' (Blanchard *et al.*, 1986). We explore its application to student learning, map the notions of power and control onto the dimensions of 'directiveness' and 'supportiveness' as used in the Blanchard model, and explain what the insights gained from this mean to us as university staff and our vision of the environment for learning.

DEFINING POWER AND CONTROL

Role power is the power that someone has because of their position in a hierarchy and which they can deploy over others from that position. People with role power are able to influence the behaviour of others because they have the necessary job or title. Lecturers have power over students because they are the lecturers, heads of departments have power over lecturers because they are heads of departments. These role power relationships are highly structured, and a description of them is the most common way of describing an organization's structure.

Personal power, on the other hand, is the power that an individual has to influence the behaviour of others because of their personality, self-confidence, charisma, or their loving, caring relationship with them. Personal power is more difficult to define than role power and is usually less well understood. It is, within our society, easier to see how to gain more role power – for example, through promotion at work – than it is to see how to acquire more personal power. 'Acquire' is, indeed, the wrong term, for whereas role power can be acquired or gained from jobs or positions, personal power is something everyone has or is capable of, but not everyone uses.

One way that individuals learn how to access and/or make better use of their personal power is through personal development. Techniques for personal development are those of counselling and therapy. Powerfulness is associated with feelings of awareness and wellbeing. People might also develop their personal powerfulness through assertiveness techniques.

The various theories of counselling and psychotherapy, upon which personal development courses are based, each have their ways of explaining personal power.

Transactional Analysis (see Harris, 1973) uses the terms 'parent', 'adult' and 'child' ego-states to describe different possible behaviours within all sorts of human relationships. At the risk of doing a complex theory a gross injustice, we think it is possible to see people operating from the parent ego-state in relationships as primarily using role power, and people acting from the adult ego-state as primarily using personal power.

Role power and personal power are different but not mutually exclusive. In most relationships there are both, and the proportion of each used varies from situation to situation. One way of representing this is as a Taggenbaum continuum as in Figure 14.1.

high ← personal power → low

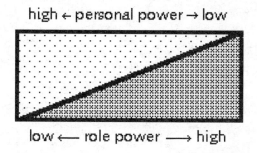

low ←— role power —→ high

Figure 14.1 *A Taggenbaum continuum*

For example, people in hierarchical working relationships can still care for each other and use personal power to influence each other. A lecturer may do something for a head of department because he or she likes him or her as a person. He or she may equally well be doing it because it pays to please the boss. The head may do something at the lecturer's suggestion because he or she respects the lecturer's opinions. Role power used entirely on its own as the way of getting someone else to do something is often a last resort and resented by the person so influenced.

People in junior hierarchical positions can also use personal power to block things, for example by saying 'no'. They can do this from the child ego-state and from the adult ego-state.

'Neuro-linguistic programming' (NLP) (see O'Connor and Seymour, 1990) is another theoretical framework for self-development. One specific application is in the giving and taking of feedback. The ability to give good feedback to others, and to learn from the feedback, is a key skill to develop to become a more effective communicator. NLP has a wonderful repertoire of slogans, one of which is 'There is no failure, only feedback', and another allied one is 'The facts are friendly'. Most people fear feedback, especially negative feedback, the effect of which is to make them feel less (personally) powerful. The ability to see feedback as neutral information (friendly facts) makes it easier to learn from it.

Carl Rogers, the author of many books on 'client-centred' counselling, was once asked how he would teach others what he knew (Rogers, 1990). His reply was that he couldn't. Client-centred therapy is an approach to counselling that sets out to minimize the (role) power difference between counsellor and client. From this perspective, he didn't like the notion of teaching, because implicit in it is the use of (teacher) role power. He could, however, create an environment where others could learn, and that was all he felt he could do. He couldn't *make* anyone learn – he therefore couldn't teach anyone anything. That was not within his (personal) power.

From the perspective of maximum role power, the lecturer is 'expert', the one who teaches others what he or she knows. From the perspective of maximum personal power, the lecturer is inspirer or facilitator of others' learning (Figure 14.2).

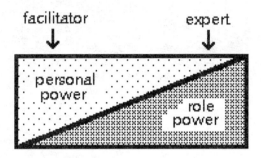

Figure 14.2 *The lecturer's personal power as facilitator*

The term 'control' is more difficult to work with. In his book on group facilitation, Heron defines the difference between power and control: 'The term "power" refers to who is doing the managerial decision-making and "control" to what procedures they use in doing it' (Heron, 1993, p.119).

Control mechanisms are associated with the deployment of role power. In the world of counselling and therapy, people 'feel in control' when they are able to influence events. This may cause them to feel more personally powerful. It may also be an effect of using personal power. The terms 'power' and 'control' are often used almost synonymously to describe a virtuous or vicious circle of interactions that affect an individual's self-confidence.

NLP, in its way of analysing communication, makes a neat distinction between a person's intentions (which are always assumed to be the best thing the person can see to do in the situation as they understand it), and the effects of their behaviour. Effects are often not what was intended. People who can see that the 'facts are friendly' can see the effects of their behaviour and separate them from their feeling about their intentions. Others, unfortunately, often defend their intentions as a means of rejecting criticism levelled at their effects.

In our experience, people who choose actions with the intention of gaining control or remaining in control of situations, often fail. Furthermore, they fail to see that the net effect of their intentions was to actually worsen the situation. This is particularly problematic if the effect required was at the personal power end of the spectrum, while the method chosen to create the effect was to use role power. The leads to what we have called the 'control paradox'.

A clear illustration of what we mean by this is the dilemma faced by parents of teenage children. They want a good relationship with their children – one they can feel in control of; one where they are pleased with the way their children do things, relate to others, etc. If they use role power (as parents) to tell their children what to do, to demand certain standards (eg 'be home before midnight', 'don't go to that party'), the intention is to regain control by getting the relationship the way they want it. The effect is, all too often, that the child resents the use of such power and the relationship with their parents deteriorates further. The paradoxical effect of being more controlling is to lose control further.

Put another way, you don't get a personal power outcome by using (predominantly) role power. The same is true, we believe, with teaching and learning. Role power can be used to control teaching, but it doesn't control learning. A certain amount of structure is required in an environment for learning. Thinking about how to structure an environment for learning led to our adaptation of the Blanchard Situational Leadership model.

Feeling in control of a relationship is the outcome, and the cause, of an effective use of personal power. It is, of course, possible for some people to feel equally in control if role power has been used to create total submission; that is, people lower down the hierarchy do what they're told out of fear of the consequences. Both types of power can lead to students respecting their tutors. Submission and fear, however, do not lead to the kind of learning universities say they want for their students, for example, to think creatively, act responsibly, be autonomous learners. Role power, we assert, cannot achieve this, and yet most lecturers see themselves as experts rather than facilitators. On induction courses for new lecturers we often ask 'What's the worst thing that could happen in a lecture?' High on the list of responses is 'that we wouldn't know the answer to a student's question'. Why does this matter? Because it's their role power, as experts, that would be challenged and seen to be lacking. The messages, and anxieties caused by those messages, as picked up by newcomers to an organization, are usually good indicators of the dominant culture within the organization.

Lecturers are more likely to feel in control of the students' learning, and be able to facilitate the kind of learning they want, if they work at getting the relationship right, and the right relationship will be one based primarily on personal power. To do that, we will need to work in ways that encourage personal development. There is already a trend in this direction. Many lecturers see personal skills development (communications skills, presentation skills, and so on) as integral parts of undergraduate programmes.

Gestalt is the name of another counselling/therapeutic model which we have found useful in working out how to develop our ideas further. The most useful concept has been 'model the process'. Another way of putting this is 'learning by example'. The application is subtle. If a lecturer leading a group notices that members of the group are not listening well to each other and wishes to draw the group's attention to this, the traditional way of doing this (using role power) is to interrupt whatever's going on and to say something like 'You're not listening to each other', with the implicit or explicit instruction to people to listen in future. A lecturer influenced by Gestalt thinking and modelling the process will not interrupt. He or she will, instead, demonstrate good listening and show that he or she is listening to participants, by, for example, reflecting back the point the participant is attempting to get others to hear – as part of the group discussion, not an interruption of it. His or her example will then set the pattern for others to follow. It is easier to facilitate through modelling the process if this is consistently demonstrated throughout the working relationship between lecturer and students.

Lecturers who primarily *tell* things to students (in lectures or formal seminars) are encouraging students to wait to be told. A group-based problem-solving curriculum is more likely to model the process, especially if the lecturer does not know the answer to the problem. To come back to our previous example, modelling the process is actually easier for the new lecturer who doesn't already know the answers to the students' questions.

BLANCHARD'S SITUATIONAL LEADERSHIP

Blanchard's Situational Leadership (Blanchard *et al.*, 1986) was originally presented as a model for supervision. It was to assist managers in deciding the appropriate form of supervision for an employee in a given circumstance. The model was also intended to contradict the commonly held view that there is one best way to manage a given person. Our adaptation of it to the supervision of learning is intended to contradict the idea that there is one best way to facilitate learning, and to propose that the structure (or control) that lecturers need to impose on a learning activity will vary according to the circumstance of the learner. This, we maintain, will lead to varied and flexible environments for learning which can be fitted into the structure of a university and also allow for personal development (for students and lecturers). It is a model that allows lecturers to choose the appropriate amount of control for the learning activity.

First, a brief overview of the model: Blanchard's model has four different activity types:

- Directing
- Coaching
- Supporting
- Delegating.

and these fit into a four-window graph with directiveness as the horizontal axis and supportiveness as the vertical axis (see Figure 14.3). The diagram, as Blanchard presents it, can be confusing as the ideal process starts in the bottom righthand corner, moves up, then across, and then down again. Quite where in the process the supervisor needs to be depends on his or her assessment of the person being supervised. As Blanchard puts it 'Different strokes for different folks!'

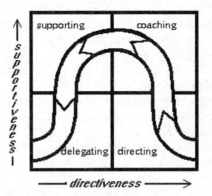

Figure 14.3 *Blanchard's Situational Leadership – the route through the four quandrants*

For any new employee (or learner), the supervisor starts by being directive, telling the new starter what to do, what the key objectives are for their work, when to report back next. As the new person begins to find their feet in the work, they will need coaching in the various skills required. Once these have been learnt and used successfully, there follows a time when the new person will still be a bit unsure of their abilities and need regular support to develop further. Finally, when the new person has both the skills and the confidence, they can be left to get on with it. The manager can delegate full responsibility to them. Subsequently, at different times, and for different reasons, the supervisor will need to operate any of the four activity types. Blanchard also offers a model for assessing employees' needs, but a knowledge of that is not required for understanding this chapter.

Running courses on learning in groups for both staff and students at the University of Bradford, we have adapted the Blanchard model to fit our role as facilitators. We start by being directive – deciding where and when the course will run, setting learning objectives, deciding on initial group exercises, and giving a structure for debriefing. In debriefing sessions we coach groups on how to give and take feedback, to improve interpersonal sensitivity and to get the balance right between achieving the task, building the team and attending to individuals (Adair's 'Action Centred Leadership' model, 1973). As the course develops we, as tutors, become progressively less directive. We ask groups to design, plan and run group exercises for each other, during which we have a supporting or advisory role. Finally, we delegate the decisions about activities and let the participant group work out for themselves what they need to do next to continue their learning as groups. Groups develop at different rates and some groups require additional coaching or more support, and the timing and extent of the delegation will vary from course to course.

In the 'directive' quadrant we are using primarily role power. As course tutors, we are deciding what will happen and when, and fitting that into the established structures of the university. In the 'coaching' quadrant we are using a lot of role power, but also some personal power – we are the experts passing on our expertise. The expertise we are passing on is in the area of interpersonal, communication skills and intended to help the learners use their personal power effectively in the learning environment we have created. In the 'supporting' quadrant we are using primarily personal power. Deciding on appropriate activities as tutors in this quadrant has become a particularly interesting subject for us, and we return to it shortly. In the 'delegating' quadrant we need to deploy little power at all. The benefit of delegating is that we don't actually have to be present while the learning is going on.

The Blanchard four-quadrant diagram can therefore be adapted to map the amount of role power deployed primarily onto the 'directiveness' axis and personal power onto the 'supportiveness' axis. The resultant mapping can be seen in Figure 14.4.

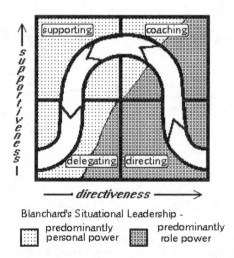

Blanchard's Situational Leadership -
predominantly personal power
predominantly role power

Figure 14.4 *Blanchard's Situational Leadership – personal power to role power*

The amount of control a lecturer has in each quadrant depends on the type of power that is being used to control things. Control based on role power is only appropriate in the directing and coaching quadrants. If the lecturer relies on role power to feel in control, then he or she will not feel in control in either the supporting or delegating quadrants. Some role power will be appropriate in the delegating quadrant, in the sense that only someone with role power has the power to delegate. The term delegation implies a (role) power to delegate. However, delegation does not lead *per se* to a feeling of being in control. People who rely predominantly on role power are often wary of delegating.

If role power is used in the supporting quadrant, the activity will become little more than just telling. At best this is a form of coaching, at worst this is directing. Supporting as an activity for lecturers can only be effective, we propose, if it is done in a non-controlling way and the only power used is personal power. If role power is used, the situation will most probably end up with the lecturer continuing to feel that he or she is 'not in control' of the activity. This can have two damaging effects. One is that the lecturer abandons the activity and resorts to more controlling (role-powerful) methods of teaching, because these are the only ones that enable him or her to feel comfortable or in control. The other is that the relationship with the students is damaged in the process – very similar, in fact, to the result of the paradoxical dilemma faced by the parent of the teenage child that we described earlier.

Our experience suggests that those lecturers (including ourselves) who are concerned to work in a less controlling way, but are not confident about how exactly to do it, or how to fit it into their work within the structures of a university course, need to be clear about:

- when it is appropriate, and hence not appropriate, to be operating in the supporting quadrant of the Blanchard model; and

- what behaviours are appropriate and inappropriate when operating in that quadrant.

Blanchard describes supporting as: 'The leader facilitates and supports subordinates' efforts toward task accomplishment and shares responsibility for decision-making with them' (Blanchard *et al.*, 1986, p.30). Our version of this would be: 'The lecturer facilitates and supports student learning and shares with them the responsibility for devising the learning activity and the method of delivery and assessment.'

We believe this is an important challenge for lecturers in higher education. We are continuing our research into the various methods by which we might appropriately and effectively support students, without losing sight of the fact that at other times we need to be able to direct, coach and delegate the learning.

For those interesting in exploring further models from counselling and therapy that can be adapted for supporting student learning, Nevis's (1987) work on organizational consulting will make interesting reading. John Heron's works on facilitating groups (1989 and 1993) are also recommended.

REFERENCES

Adair, J (1973) *Action Centred Leadership*, McGraw Hill, London.
Blanchard, K, Zigarmi, P and Zigarmi, D (1986) *Leadership and the One-Minute Manager*, Collins, London.
Harris, T A (1973) *I'm OK – You're OK*, Pan Books, London.
Heron, J (1989) *The Facilitator's Handbook*, Kogan Page, London.
Heron, J (1993) *Group Facilitation*, Kogan Page, London.
Nevis, E C (1987) *Organizational Consulting: A Gestalt Approach*, Gardner Press, New York.
O'Connor, J and Seymour, J (1990) *Introducing Neuro-Linguistic Programming*, Crucible Books, London.
Rogers, C (1990) *The Carl Rogers Reader*, Constable, London.

SECTION IV
Staff Development Approaches and Methods

Chapter 15

Reducing Stress in Teaching and Learning

Stephen Cox and Ruth Heames

INTRODUCTION

> 'Is this the last straw? Again and again since 1981 the funding screw has been tightened on universities. In the last five years alone the amount of money for each student has gone down by 25%. Over the life of the Conservative Government it must now, with this week's further 12% cut, over three years have been reduced by at least half in real terms.' (*The Times Higher*, 1.12.95)

Stress is a normal part of life and living. A certain amount of stress is often necessary to stimulate peak performance. Selye (1956), coined the term 'eustress' for this. On the other hand, a lack of challenge or stimulus can be as stressful as too much stress. There are some indications that too great a level of stress can be linked to an excessive workload, either in terms of having too much to do, or having too many work roles to fulfil (Fisher, 1994). However, other important factors contribute to a potentially harmful level of stress for some individuals. Although there is little data for higher education, a recent study by Stead *et al.* (1995), examined stress levels of further education teachers. They investigated the influence of factors such as 'degree of consultation by management', 'the quality of communication', 'the working environment', 'the ability to produce quality work' and 'general job satisfaction', on the stress levels of these teachers. Their findings are striking. Among the 380 teachers on a multi-site college of further education, 20% scored at 'clinical' and 23% at 'borderline clinical' levels of free-floating anxiety. A healthy workforce would contain about 10% scoring at clinical levels (Stead, 1996). Major factors leading to poor decision-making as a symptom of over-stress for these teachers were:

- the inability to provide quality teaching;
- rates of pay;
- industrial relations between management and workers – particularly 'lack of management consultation'.

Employers have a 'duty of care' to ensure that employees are not subjected to the risk of psychiatric damage (Palmer, 1995). Over-stress can cause physical as well as mental health problems. Fisher (1994) in her chapter on 'Life, stress and health', demonstrates a clear relationship between psychological state and health. She goes on to discuss some of the likely causes of stress for both staff and students in higher education.

Teachers have had to adjust to the major changes that have been imposed upon them in the last few years. These have not merely demanded extra work, but have also made additional demands. These changes have altered the nature of some of the roles that teachers are expected to undertake. Student numbers have increased dramatically without a matching increase in the numbers of teachers. Appraisal and performance related pay, quality audit and assessment, have also become an integral part of the system. The move to modularity in many universities seems to have led to a mushrooming of bureaucracy. Part-time and short contract teachers have been appointed who do not have the obligation or the commitment to take on pastoral, research, consultative or administrative duties. These then pose an additional burden for the proportionately fewer full-time staff who remain.

Too often, therefore, teachers find themselves faced with much to do, and too little time in which to do it. This leads to problematic levels of stress that affect teachers' professional and personal lives adversely.

Students have also been placed under increasing stress. The transition for post-school students from small tightly knit, closely supervised groups studying three or four subjects, to different large groups of 100 or more in each of up to eight modules can be very traumatic. They now have greater financial problems than ever before, and are taught in larger groups, often working on their own or with their peers for long periods without the direct support of a member of staff.

Thus in considering the impact of change on today's universities, it is now evident that institutions and the people in them can no longer continue to operate in ways that have sufficed until now. Indeed, it might be detrimental to do so: detrimental to the staff, the students and to the institutions themselves.

Handy (1989) mentions the human tendency to make a continuing series of minor adjustments to the way we do things so as to accommodate to the pressures of current and impending changes. Many teachers find themselves in this position. Through a continual series of small adjustments over the years in response to pressures in their environment, they find themselves in a new and in some cases, potentially life-threatening situation. One restorative strategy might be to adopt carefully thought out strategies and practices that are compatible with our new and considerably changed surroundings.

There are some practical ways in which teachers can manage their teaching and therefore their stress levels more effectively. In addition, there are some principles and practices that might help teachers to help their students to manage their stress (Cox and Heames, in preparation).

TEACHING TECHNIQUES THAT CAN REDUCE TEACHERS' STRESS

Teachers in higher education are normally appointed for their subject expertise rather than for their ability or interest in teaching. The increase in the number and diversity of their students can make traditional assumptions and practices about teaching obsolete, or even ineffective for both teachers and students.

For instance, it used to be conventional practice to require students to complete a series of essays or laboratory reports or similar work at monthly intervals or so during a course. This was reasonable with small classes. With classes of a hundred or more students, the time required to assess one essay from each student can consume 50 hours of staff time – well over the normal expectation for a complete working week. Multiply this by the three, four or five essays a year that used to be associated with traditional courses and it is obvious that the assessment load become less and less sustainable as student numbers rise. What is needed is a complete rethink of assessment practices to accommodate to the new climate of large classes, and often multiple modules within courses.

This requires some fundamental questions, such as what is assessment for? Is it simply to generate a set of coursework or examination scores by which to sort students into degree categories? Or is it at least in part a learning process to provide students with clear and relatively current information about their progress and their strengths and weaknesses? There are other questions, too. How far do we wish to assess the development of skills in students? If we wish to do so, how is this best done, and do we integrate this process with assessment of academic attainment, or do we attempt to do it separately? Depending upon the answers, different strategies might well be appropriate.

Once we have begun to address these and similar questions, we can begin to select the appropriate methods to suit our aims. At the same time we can adopt or invent methods of assessment that allow us to handle the work from the new, larger classes in a way that reduces the time and the stress that could accompany the use of traditional methods in new circumstances (see Gibbs, 1992)

Similar principles can be applied to our approaches to the methods of working with our subject material. For instance, teachers can choose to move towards resource-based learning. This need not, indeed should not normally, involve creating large amounts of new learning material from scratch. Trying to do this is likely to increase stress levels that are already too high. Instead teachers might identify existing textbooks or appropriate learning material available from elsewhere. American texts sometimes come with extensive support materials, such as computer-aided learning packages, multiple-choice question banks and study guides – all tried and tested, albeit in America. (For an example of this approach, see Case Study 2 in Cox and Gibbs, 1994.) The Open Learning foundation publishes a growing portfolio of resource-based learning material in a UK context.

Another approach might be to concentrate on devising problems for students to work on, either individually, or in groups. These can range from simple worked examples to case studies lasting a whole module or course.

There are potential pitfalls in moving towards resource-based learning. One is the danger that students become even more isolated. Teachers contemplating a move in this direction might wish to consider steps they can take to provide the 'social glue' that bonds students into cohesive groups. Frequent seminars, peer support or study groups, and a reappraisal of the nature and purpose of lectures, are some strategies that can address this issue (Cox and Gibbs, 1994).

TEACHING TECHNIQUES THAT CAN REDUCE STUDENTS' STRESS

For many students, unnecessary levels of stress can be caused by uncertainty, especially at the beginning of their studies. This can be uncertainty about roles and expectations; uncertainty about the level, volume and quality of written and other work that will be required of them; and uncertainty about the social and organizational contexts in which they will be expected to work.

It is within the teacher's capacity to reduce greatly this uncertainty and the stress caused, by simply addressing the issues. This can be done partly by the way in which he or she behaves and partly through the induction and skills development tasks he or she introduces.

The induction period offers an unrepeatable opportunity to establish a sound communication system and a group identity at course and module level. This is also the appropriate time for the lecturer and the group to set the ground rules within which the learning experience will take place; to develop an understanding of team roles and behaviour, and to begin to come to terms with the nature of the academic demands of the course.

Burton and Dimbleby (1988) suggest that 'the self is at the beginning and end of all communication'. Students and teachers must therefore take individual responsibility for their contribution to the learning experience. If either or both parties are not open or comfortable in their communications, the range and quality of the learning experience will be restricted and probably stressful. Generating a positive climate with an open communication system is another essential task for the teacher. Ice-breaking activities such as those found in life-skills and management texts help to remove barriers and build positive working relationships within classes and between students and teachers. They give students permission to get to know one another and help them to feel less overwhelmed and anxious about who they are going to work with over a significant period of their lives.

Managing the learning environment also involves facilitating a set of individuals into a cohesive group. Therefore, team building is essential to reduce feelings of tension and stress as each group progresses through the forming and norming stages. The teacher therefore needs to understand and address group dynamics and to implement strategies to ensure that group conflict and tension are minimized. In this way, self-appointed 'experts' and the more assertive students can be harmoniously assimilated into the group, reducing stress for everyone concerned.

The teachers' attitude and style of management are also influential in establishing a positive climate. It is essential to be fair, open and non-judgemental. Hidden agendas on the part of the teacher – for instance, being uncertain, unclear or unwilling to discuss criteria – can create tension, barriers and stress.

It is also important to be explicit about the nature or the respective roles of teacher and student in the learning process. With increasing student numbers and a less than proportionate increase in staff, students need to be ever more independent in their approaches to learning. Such independence can be overwhelming and various types of preparatory work are necessary to provide students with a set of principles and a framework within which to operate. Thus it is a positive investment to address explicitly the roles and expectations of students at an early stage in a course of study. Addressing students' anxieties, practical concerns and common issues within the group can be of great help in alleviating the need for students to seek staff outside class time for reassurance and guidance. This in turn can help to reduce pressure and stress on both staff and students.

Another important issue associated with the formation and development of roles within a group are the codes of behaviour that are expected from both students and staff. Groundrules can be generated by consensus to cover timeliness, the nature and extent of seminar contributions, and so on. This clarity is a positive way forward to ease tension within the group.

In the early stages of a programme, the teacher needs to set the learning agenda for the group of students. Course documents can be overwhelming for students. A module or course outline with a syllabus, reading list and weekly schedule of topics and a guide to independent study tasks, can be far more effective in reassuring and supporting students through their work. If necessary, this can be written in a graduated form, providing a lot of support in the early stages, and gradually providing less and less as the students become more confident and competent.

Looking forward, graduates of the future will require a greater range of skills or capabilities for the marketplace. Cognitive skills alone will not be sufficient to ensure survival. Interpersonal skills, communicating with individuals and groups will be indispensable. Creative, innovative and problem-solving approaches will enable individuals to become more adept at the work they undertake, and thus become more attractive to prospective employers. An individual's ability to identify his or her own learning needs and the skills to discover sources of help and to learn independently will be even more essential as mainstream careers and jobs become less and less common (Winter, 1995).

If these skills have the potential to enable individuals to cope in the workplace then they have the potential to help students to progress through the process of higher education and gain intrinsic as well as extrinsic rewards for the sustained investment in themselves over a three-year period in a stressful environment.

With this is mind, teachers might wish to take on the role of facilitator, rather than the more traditional role of teacher. Assisting students to develop their self-awareness will enable them in turn to recognize their own life stressors, roles and learning styles, thereby allowing them to be more selective in the methods of learning they choose.

Encouraging students to use reflective techniques in learning will enable them to become more evaluative, creative and effective in problem solving. With such abilities, new knowledge becomes less threatening and the work less stressful for students as they have both a framework from which to operate and a set of guiding principles. It is acknowledged that effective communication is fundamental to the quality of a learning experience. Therefore students need to be able to listen effectively to both the teacher and their peers, and to be able to negotiate when there are unresolved issues and conflicting opinions. Students also need to be assertive in their approach to managing the workload and their own learning. These skills, while fundamental, are not always well developed in students. From the beginning of a course it might be prudent to create opportunities for students to develop and acquire these skills.

For instance, while developing time-management skills as a practical solution to help students to cope with their workload, it might also be appropriate to encourage them to develop a longer-term perspective for life. Students need to be encouraged to create a balanced life style, for it is a means of establishing good health and wellbeing. Goal setting can be a means not only of accomplishing practical tasks, but also taking a planned approach to the future, in order to work towards satisfying individual needs, and achieving positive outcomes.

SOURCES OF HELP FOR TEACHERS

Teaching in higher education can be a lonely and an isolating activity, as well as a very stressful one. This can be true for newcomers and long-serving teachers alike. Despite the growth of staff development and similar units that run workshops where colleagues can meet to discuss developments in teaching and learning, it can be inconvenient or intimidating to attend them. However, help is at hand, in the form of potential support from colleagues. This can take a variety of forms, depending upon local circumstances and the needs of individuals. One approach that can be very effective is to team up with a trusted colleague or colleagues. Some organizations even make formal provision for mentorships or peer professional development partnerships. Whether the structures are formal or informal, colleagues are almost invariably one of the best sources of support. In today's overstretched and sometimes confrontational institutional systems, colleagues very often band together for mutual support in this way as a response to the uncongenial nature of the systems in which they work.

It might be appropriate to begin by identifying simple and relatively undemanding forms of mutual support. One person might agree to attend the classes of another and to comment afterwards on certain aspects of their operation agreed beforehand. Another might offer to share some teaching in return for help with designing assessments. Whatever the arrangements, the fact that some of the load is shared is important, as is the discussion of teaching issues that will inevitably result.

In some cases the stress might be so severe that it is necessary to get help more formally from the organization. Any higher education institution will have a personnel or similar department that will run courses on time or stress management for instance, perhaps even bespoke courses for a group of colleagues. There will also be access to a welfare officer or similar and perhaps even stress counselling in some cases, although this is unusual.

Individuals under extreme pressure might consider approaching their line manager. This may or may not be an effective strategy, depending on the rapport and management skills that such a person deploys. The decision about whom to approach for help can be a very tricky one.

An officer of the local branch of one of the teaching unions can be very helpful, and an increasing number have training in first-line help for over-stressed colleagues. It is likely that to support any meeting with an official, the person concerned will be asked to write down a summary of the causes of their stress and any action that they have taken to alleviate it. This can be a very therapeutic exercise in itself, as can the act of talking freely about it to a relatively neutral person.

CONCLUSION

Over-stress is becoming more and more common among higher education teachers, and is rising in frequency for their students. There are some common factors and some common solutions. Ultimately, teachers retain the overall responsibility for taking action to control their own stress levels and to help their students develop the skills and attributes that will in turn stand them in good stead in coping with the stresses of life and work.

REFERENCES

Burton, G and Dimbleby, R (1988) *Between Ourselves*, Edward Arnold, London.

Cox, S and Gibbs, G (1994) *Course Design for Resource Based Learning in Social Science*, Oxford Centre for Staff Development, Oxford.

Cox, S and Heames, R (in preparation) *53 Practical Ideas to Reduce Stress in Teaching and Learning*.

Fisher, S (1994) *Stress in Academic Life*, SRHE/Open University Press, Buckingham.

Gibbs, G (1992) *Assessing More Students*, Oxford Centre for Staff Development, Oxford.

Handy, C (1989) *The Age of Unreason*, Penguin, Harmondsworth.

Palmer, S (1995) 'Legal Aspects of Occupational Stress', *Counselling Psychology Review*, **10**, 4.

Selye, H (1956) *The Stress of Life*, Longmans Green, London.

Stead, B, Fletcher, B and Jones, F (1995) 'Relationships Between Workload, Cognitive Decision Making and Psychological Well-being', Unpublished paper presented at the Occupational Psychology Conference.

Stead B (1996) Private correspondence.

Winter, J (1995) *Skills for Graduates in the 21st Century*, Association of Graduate Recruiters.

Chapter 16

Reinventing Lecturers, Students and Learning Programmes

Paul Gentle

INTRODUCTION

This chapter will argue that the arrival of the neo-industrial age is bringing about a change in the culture of British universities. This centres around the need for institutions to gain competitive advantage in the national and international marketplace. As a consequence, academic staff now need to engage in radical innovations in learning and teaching.

A model of staff development is proposed which enables academic departments to add value to their students' learning experience. This adding of value can only occur if students are regarded as partners, or co-producers in the processes of higher education (HE). It will fail if the metaphor is of students as customers.

The proposed staff development model implies that universities should become learning organizations in three dimensions: institutional management; personal and professional development; curriculum design and content.

MANAGEMENT IN A LEARNING ORGANIZATION

The ethos of managerialism, which many contemporary HE institutions have attempted to harness in order to fuel corporate ambitions, may not provide the most helpful model for meeting the challenges of global society and cultures. Scott and Watson (1994, p.43) have identified what they call a 'managerial' approach in universities and colleges with between 7,000 and 15,000 students (the vast majority of all universities in the UK). Below 5,000 students, a 'collegial' style of management, familiar to most who knew the HE system before the late 1980s, is more likely to prevail.

It is the 'managerial' approach that has borne the brunt of criticism from those who argue that resource-limited expansion in HE mitigates against the tenets of humanistic educational processes. It has brought with it a world of supposedly business-based notions of mission statements, core activities, customers and service providers, and in so doing has established a model suitable for an industrial age. More specifically, it has many characteristics in common with what Goodman (1995, p.16) defines as 'the product/service design-oriented time' of the 1960s and 1970s.

However, the increasing importance of knowledge-based industries has, in business, created:

> 'the value-oriented time [which] heralds the transition to a new wealth-creating age – the neo-industrial age... Such an age is marked by an ever-accelerating pace of competition in which "customers" value expectations will increase, putting greater and greater pressure on organisations' innovative performance.' (Goodman, 1995)

A more creative and proactive form of management is implied by such changes, and has been identified by Scott and Watson in institutions with more than 15,000 students. They call this a 'strategic' approach in which institutional hierarchies become flatter, and where layers of management are replaced by loosely coupled networks. They call for 'a reinterpretation and recombination of both the collegial and managerial approaches to meet the radically different challenge of managing mass institutions' (1994, p.43).

With sensitive reinterpretation, institutions could build on collegial traditions of 'academic and pastoral intimacy... [to provide] a flexible context in which... learning contracts can be negotiated... it offers a creative environment which, at its best, fosters student learning rather than rote teaching' (*ibid*.).

This emphasis aligns with the broad definition of quality in HE offered by Harvey:

> 'In relation to teaching and learning, transformative quality sees the student as a participant in the learning process. It focuses on the enhancement and empowerment of the learner through a learning experience that adds value and equips the participant for lifelong learning.' (1996, p.23)

It also corresponds to the vision of the learning organization now increasingly prevalent in knowledge-based industries.

What is a learning organization like? According to Pedler *et al.* (1988), a learning organization is one that:

- has a climate in which individual members are encouraged to learn and to develop their full potential;
- extends this learning culture to include customers, suppliers and other significant stakeholders;

- makes human resource development strategy central to business policy;
- is in a continuous process of organizational transformation.

(Pedler et al. quoted in Dale, 1994, p.24)

As definitive knowledge-based organizations, universities could benefit substantially by demonstrating awareness of what enables businesses to engage in processes of continuous transformation. That awareness is already present in aspirations to student-centred learning which are embodied in institutional philosophies. But unless it translates itself into management strategies that empower HE organizations through staff development, such aspirations are unlikely to be fulfilled.

KEYS TO REINVENTION

The argument to be developed in the following pages hinges on the following premises:

- Students are not the customers of higher education. ('Students are not simply consumers of education. They are also producers of it. Student effort is fundamental to HE', Fitzgerald, 1996, p.12.)
- HE institutions should resemble the cutting-edge organizations in which our students aspire to work. ('The governing metaphor is the student-as-worker', Beare *et al.*, 1989, p.64.)
- Students and staff in HE institutions should be encouraged to develop self-reliance, innovation and creative thinking, *actively.*
- Employers and other societal stakeholders are in a strong position to gauge, and offer constructive criticism on, the outputs of HE. ('Students and employers will increasingly exert their claims on the content, process, pedagogical relationships and outcomes of the curriculum', Middlehurst and Barnett, 1994, p.58.)

If students are active producers within HE institutions, and are effectively colleagues of academic and support staff, there are clearly enormous implications for student recruitment, mutual expectations of the processes of teaching and learning, and the development and implementation of programmes of learning.

CREATING THE CONTEXT

As a result of some years' experience of consultancy in the field of foreign language training, I have seen at first hand the powerful effects of applying concepts from strategic management and creative management to educational settings. Only since early 1995, however, have I felt sufficiently confident to attempt to implement some of these concepts in the institution in which I work. It is to the credit of the University of Central Lancashire that an academic department is empowered to a significant extent to establish its own culture, within a broader context of the university's mission.

The preliminary case study outlined below sets out the ways in which the reinvention of curriculum design and content can feed into staff development strategies at departmental level. This is followed by some thoughts on how senior management can provide strategic support for an institution as a whole.

The Department of Languages at the University of Central Lancashire is one of the largest in the institution, with 680 FTE students (1995/96) and over 50 lecturing staff (some of whom are part-time, paid hourly). In the early months of 1996, it was the subject of an assessment visit by the Higher Education Funding Council for England (HEFCE). This very factor acted as a catalyst for much developmental activity during the months preceding the visit, and drew together previously disparate language subject teams under a banner of 'departmentality'. The department benefited substantially from arguing successfully for a joint visit, assessing together all ten languages currently offered.

Attempts at goal-setting for the department as a whole had begun during its infancy, since from 1990/91 it was established from the language-providing arms of two antecedent organizations (the School of Office Communication and Languages, and the former Faculty of Arts). Although discussions, typically at biannual department awaydays, had always been constructive and informed by the views both of senior members of staff and of new recruits to the department, they had not resulted in commonly shared objectives or actions which might shape the department's future.

In 1994/95, the following key decisions were taken by the departmental management team which provided the bedrock for departmental change.

- Publish indicative, criterion-referenced assessment guidelines for staff and students, across a range of ten assessment task types.
- Devise and implement a departmental first-year induction programme, to highlight learner autonomy and the use of IT/multimedia language learning facilities.
- Create, after widespread consultation with staff and students, a departmental Learning Policy.
- Establish a series of final-year dissertation workshops across the department.
- Launch a voluntary programme of peer observation of teaching.

- Provide a channel for communication and dissemination of ideas on teaching and learning through a departmental newsletter.
- Run an annual 10-week Staff Training Programme for all lecturers.

Up to and including this period, the department had received strong support from the university-wide Enterprise in Higher Education programme, a factor which in itself had started to bring about a culture change in some areas of the department. Two specific projects contributed firmly to the new department's infrastructure: first, a student-written guide for the 2,000 students per year who benefit from the institution-wide Electives programme for non-specialist linguists; and second, a student-devised self-access induction pack for users of the Language Learning Centre.

It is important to note the above developments as prerequisite to the process of reinvention of the roles of staff, students and learning programmes, since they provide tangible examples of successful change in progress and are thus already empowering factors in terms of staff awareness of the creative contribution which lecturers and students can make to institutional change. Referring back to Pedler's definition of a learning organization, it is essential for individual members to learn and thus to maximize the chances to develop their full potential.

CREATIVE PROBLEM-SOLVING

One aspect of the legacy of the department's history that was most difficult to change was the range of different cultures for the structure and conceptualization of the curriculum. Champions of innovation and change existed within every major language subject, each intent on promoting their respective enthusiasms, but prevented from contextualizing this within the work of the department as a whole. This led to fascinating but sporadic initiatives on incorporating IT, exploiting self-access facilities, peer and self-assessment, simulations and project work, involving employers in the student experience, teaching study skills and essay writing, and so on. The section of the HEFCE assessment report on the department's curriculum offering identified the need to focus more clearly across all languages on student learning outcomes at higher levels of study.

It was clear by 1994/95 that an ad hoc approach to change by example was too evolutionary and unchannelled for the department's desired short-term aim of externally recognized excellence in teaching and learning (through a successful HEFCE visit outcome), and for its long-term need to survive and prosper in an increasingly competitive environment. A more radical view would need to be created, and shared, if the department were to reinvent itself as a learning organization. With the active leadership and support of the head of department, a broad goal and vision had to be defined in order to create a set of guiding metaphors for the development of the department over the next four or five years.

The start of the academic session 1995/96 provided the opportunity for further supporting measures for strategic change.

- Meetings of all departmental staff, previously restricted to awaydays twice a year, became fortnightly.

- Commitment was made by the head of department to review all individual staff timetabled duties allocations in the light of eventual strategic commitments by the department.

- Eight students were employed as part-time language learning assistants in the Language Learning Centre, with a specific brief to sit on the departmental Materials Development Group. This gave students an unprecedented role in the operational management of the department's work.

- The university's Training and Development section was commissioned to provide training on team leadership for the 13 members of the departmental management team.

In order to break with the tradition of meetings as bureaucratic formalities, it was decided to design a format for the fortnightly staff meetings which would allow for widespread participation, for creativity, and for the modelling of techniques and approaches which participants might themselves wish to transfer into the learning situations which they were responsible for managing. This led to a regular 'Big Issue' slot, taking at least half of the total meeting time, with some pre-planned inputs from a wide variety of contributors (including students). The chairing of meetings rotated on a voluntary basis, allowing the head of department to participate more equitably in discussion, and enabling lecturers to gain experience of a valuable personal transferable skill.

The fifth meeting, in November 1995, was designed exclusively as a staff development workshop, embodying many of the principles of 'creative management' (Goodman, 1995) or 'management creativity' (Proctor, 1995). These involve the premise that 'managers... need to discover new and better ways to solve problems... Creativity... helps to encourage profitable innovations, rekindles employee motivation and improves personal skills and team performance' (Proctor, 1995, p.2).

The meeting was extremely well attended and had one overall objective – to develop commonly shared statements on ways in which the department might prepare itself for the year 2000 and beyond. The workshop used the following stages, all adapted from the Creative Problem-Solving toolkit suggested by Goodman (1995, p.81). This comprises a checklist of activities ('tools') which are appropriate to the problem-solving 'functions' of: problem evaluation; idea generation; imagineering; selection; realization. Goodman suggests that the toolkit is particularly effective in generating a climate of lateral thinking, off-the-wall suggestions and the joy and energy of synergistic group work. So attractive is the picture he portrays of a creatively empowered organization, it was impossible not to want to experiment using his ideas.

- **Stage 1.** Deep-breathing relaxation activity.
- **Stage 2.** Relating pictorial images (Museum of the Mind) to the department.
- **Stage 3.** Developing scenarios for the HE environment of the year 2000: social, technological, economic and political dimensions.
- **Stage 4.** Group sentence-building of potential aspiration statements, beginning 'The Department of Languages...' (each member of a circle of 6–8 staff added one word at a time to a slip of paper passed round).
- **Stage 5.** Evaluation of selected aspiration statements.

It is worth noting here that previous workshops (in staff seminars and at awaydays) had drawn on many of the techniques in Goodman's toolkit, since these already form part of the repertoire of learning activities in foreign language education. It is particularly striking that a half-hour visualizing session, based on 'wishful thinking' projections, in July 1994, was referred to anecdotally many times by individual lecturers over subsequent months as having made powerful impressions on colleagues' mutual understanding of their role and position in the department, and of its future direction and relevance to collective goals.

The specific outcomes of the November 1995 session set the future agendas for many subsequent meetings, discussions and actions. The scenario-building (Stage 3) revealed no great surprises, but built coherently on current trends both in the department and societally, and emphasized the ongoing decline in public resourcing of HE and the growing implications of global regionalism. This latter raised the crucial question of the need to offer greater provision of languages appropriate to the Asia Pacific region. There was also recognition of the demand to equip students for lifelong learning, and to enhance their capability to add value to the employers with whom they might wish to work.

It might have been assumed, in the light of the brief group feedback talks given on the respective environmental dimensions, that the ensuing aspiration sentences (Stage 4) would have addressed issues of curriculum design and quality enhancement in explicit terms. The six sentences which attracted most widespread support (all were 'voted on' from a total of 15 sentences, and were endorsed by between 22% and 100% of participants) focused only indirectly on such issues. The overwhelming message which emerged from the sentence statements was of the imperative for empowerment through staff development. The sentences appear below, with italicization of those words which indicate a tendency for apparent flippancy to distort the serious intent of some statements.

The Department of Languages...

- should not be aiming at the lowest possible denominator but at leading the way for language teaching and learning;
- should adapt from being a teaching establishment to being (not only that) but a *happy one*;
- should change its approach to staff development;
- will manage its staff/develop staff potential in various ways such as giving new incentives, more encouragement and *more money*;
- aims to develop more skilful lecturers by improving its standard pedagogical support through enabling more staff to *spend freely*.

The partial emphasis here on financial empowerment can be explained by the recent introduction (in October 1995) of devolved identification of spending priorities to language subject teams.

Subsequent sessions involved sentence transformation activities to refine the statements and build them into a strategic plan for the department, based on:

- Exceeding stakeholders' expectations of graduates of the department.
- Becoming a recognized international leader in those applications of language pedagogy in which the department excels.
- Using staff appraisal as a means of identifying individuals' contributions, through staff development, to the achievement of the department's plan.
- Equitable distribution of workloads so as to create a variety of career paths in the department.

ACADEMIC CAREERS

The notion of a range of career paths parallels discussion under way during 1995/96 at institutional level on the role of the Principal Lecturer post in a 'new university'. Concern was expressed by the Pro-Vice-Chancellor (Staffing) over the apparent difficulty of recognizing excellence in lecturers in the domain of teaching and learning.

This corresponds to the widely published views of academics such as Gibbs, who argues that attempts to recognize and improve the quality of teaching should parallel the processes of enhancing the outputs of research activity. He outlines a series of measures to achieve such recognition, varying from 'cooperative teaching in teams… presenting accounts of teaching in progress… peer review of teaching' to 'peer review of course proposals' (1995, p.151).

The swell of discussion on the recognition of teaching and learning as being at least as important as that of research suggests at least two readily identifiable alternative career paths for academics in HE: lecturer as specialist in research, lecturer as specialist in teaching and learning. The Department of Languages would wish to add a third path to the range of possibilities (while in no way limiting the entire career development of any one individual to a single exclusive path): that of the lecturer as manager/entrepreneur, capable of participating in and leading developmental and strategic initiatives.

Timetable allocations are now based on lecturers constructing a balance of activities which are given tariff values in each of the career path areas.

While the primary onus of department staff development is on individually negotiated personal development planning (as has always been the case under appraisal schemes), it is now with concrete reference to a commonly owned strategy. The individual's identity is now reinforced by being placed in the context of growth and development of a project team (which may be conceived simultaneously as a subsection of the department, and as the department as a whole). The academic-led emphasis on staff development has created an atmosphere in which lecturers can feel supported by the departmental management team, and work directly, in the next phase of development, on curriculum design and content. The very focus on professional development of staff will pave the way effectively for curriculum development with a similar focus. Hounsell predicts an optimistic scenario in which students take more responsibility for their own learning, suggesting that:

> 'it can help to set intellectual challenges which extend beyond content to processes of learning and teaching, and it nudges students towards becoming more versatile and resourceful learners – a capability which they will need if they are to go on renewing and updating their knowledge in the years beyond graduation.' (Hounsell, 1994, p.92)

Only if staff are empowered in an equivalent manner can they be agents in the effective empowerment of students. Gibbs says convincingly that 'in all institutions if improving the quality of teaching is going to engage academics on any long-term basis then it has to challenge them intellectually' (1995, p.156).

The logical next step for the Department of Languages is to reinvent programmes of learning in order to create the intellectual challenges which enable students and staff to engage actively in continuous transformation. This occurs through a further process of creative problem-solving in which the department identifies a vision of an idealized state towards which it can work collectively. The problem-solving approach is needed to address the filling of the gaps between current and desired practices.

The key to learning is through benchmarking as a means to evaluation of actions taken, and as a means to gaining inspiration from successes elsewhere in education (and beyond, to other knowledge-based sectors).

INSTITUTION-WIDE IMPLICATIONS

If departmental activity as outlined above forms the base for reinventing the university as a genuine learning organization, there must also be two further layers added to form a pyramid if the paradigm of reinvention is to be complete:

- institutional staff development policy and practice;
- resource and moral commitment by senior managers.

Departmental autonomy is always constrained by institutional requirements and control mechanisms, and is always dependant on benign support at Faculty level and above. Furthermore, if change is predicated entirely on departmental activity, there must be a strong chance that it may never materialize. There is clear evidence to support the case that an institutional vision for change in a core activity such as teaching and learning is instrumental to real change in practice. Thorne (1995) has advocated massive increases in spending on specific training and development programmes for teaching and learning at the University of Sunderland, and has created mechanisms to reward innovation and excellence through fixed-term Teaching and Learning Fellowships (1995).

CONCLUSION

While cynicism is often the response of academics to industrial-style training programmes, it is only in making staff development central to the strategic policies of universities that they can hope to develop their own distinctive and truly pervasive learning cultures. The key lies in Gibbs's assertion that 'intellectual rigour and scholarship' must be applied to quality enhancement at every level. Creative problem-solving is both empowering and intellectually challenging – as well as being a powerful means of ensuring the survival of our institutions in a global environment.

The department of the year 2000 and beyond, then, could genuinely be one to which students apply as if for a career post, and are entitled to equivalent professional development activities as their lecturing colleagues who conceive of themselves as managers of learning. Their products are developed jointly, both in the form of the research and development activities and the graduates they offer to the community – value-adding in the broadest sense of the term.

REFERENCES

Beare, H, Caldwell, B and Millikan, R (1989) *Creating an Excellent School,* Routledge, London.

Dale, M (1994) 'Learning Organizations' in *Managing Learning,* C Maben and P Iles (eds), Routledge, London.

Fitzgerald, M (1996) 'No Mark for Effort Skews Assessment', *The Times Higher Education Supplement,* 5 April 1996, p.12.

Gibbs, G (1995) 'Quality in Research and in Teaching', *Quality in Higher Education,* **1**, 2, pp.147–57.

Goodman, M (1995) *Creative Management,* Prentice Hall, London.

Harvey, L (1996) 'Question of Definition', *Managing HE,* **1**, 2, pp.22–5.

Hounsell, D (1994) 'Educational Development', in *Managing the University Curriculum,* J Bocock and D Watson (eds), Open University Press, Milton Keynes.

Middlehurst, R and Barnett, R (1994) 'Changing the Subject: The Organization of Knowledge and Academic Culture', in *Managing the University Curriculum,* J Bocock and D Watson (eds), Open University Press, Milton Keynes.

Pedler, M, Boydell, T and Burgoyne, J (1988) *Learning Company Project Report,* Training Agency, Sheffield.

Proctor, T (1995) *The Essence of Management Creativity,* Prentice Hall, London.

Scott, P and Watson, D (1994) Managing the Curriculum: Roles and Responsibilities', in *Managing the University Curriculum,* J Bocock and D Watson (eds), Open University Press, Milton Keynes.

Thorne, M (1995) 'Nudges and Winks: Searching for a model of staff development which supports a strategic approach to institutional changes in teaching and learning', Paper given at SEDA Conference, University of Sunderland, 18–19 December 1995.

Chapter 17

Some Issues Impacting on University Teaching and Learning: Implications for Academic Developers

Philip C Candy

INTRODUCTION

In the past few years, higher education in many countries throughout the world has undergone dramatic and far-reaching change. Factors such as:

- institutional mergers and amalgamations;
- huge increases in enrolments and in class sizes;
- reduced funding per student;
- greater concentration on linkages with the world of work and responsiveness to the demands of industry and the professions;
- dissatisfaction with progression rates, especially in higher degree studies;
- more diverse and demanding student groups; and
- increased pressures for institutions to submit themselves to public scrutiny and to account more carefully for the quality of their activities (and of their graduates);

have all combined to increase the complexity of academic work. The following quote from a feature article in a Canadian newspaper poses a series of hypothetical questions which give a sense of some additional new directions:

> 'What if universities were privately owned? What if they were listed on the stock exchanges? What if professors held shares? What if universities could open new franchises, take over others, go out of business and start again? What if a "university" no longer meant a vast sprawl of concrete blocks on several square kilometres of suburban tundra, with residences and sportsplexes and boards of governors and student unions and an army of support staff to run them all, but rather small partnerships of entrepreneurial professors?

'What if classes were held on the Internet? What if fees were deregulated, tenure abolished and specialization – among institutions as among professors – encouraged? What if universities operated all year round? What if a university's revenues depended on how much its students earned after graduation? What if a professor's pay depended on how well his [or her] students were taught? What if, in short, universities worked very differently than they do now?' (Coyne, 1996)

The fact is that every one of these scenarios has already come to pass. Although much of higher education provision is still recognisably based on traditional models, it also true that initiatives such as these are no longer simply futuristic possibilities, but are already realities for staff, students and administrators in at least some places. And it is also a fact that such initiatives are no longer on the fringe of conventional higher education, but are increasingly invading its core.

Not unexpectedly, major changes such as these have not gone unchallenged, and I am not intending in this chapter to suggest that academics, or academic developers for that matter, should meekly acquiesce to changes that may be regarded as threatening the integrity of the field. Indeed, to the contrary, there is a duty of care on academics to speak up against those changes which they see as antithetical to the very qualities that make higher education higher in the first place. By the same token, however, there is little point in pretending that such transformations are not happening or that they are simply likely to go away. The topography of higher education is changing rapidly, significantly and, it would appear, irreversibly, and this has clear implications for staff and educational development professionals.

The purpose of this chapter is to explore a limited number of such changes and to consider some of the challenges which they are likely to pose as we confront the 21st century. Clearly, it is not possible in a short chapter such as this to deal with more than a few of the many changes that are impacting on higher education. I have chosen to discuss the following seven issues, before turning to a brief consideration of their likely implications for staff and educational developers:

- widespread availability of computer-based access to information;
- increasing diversity in the student body;
- the demand to learn off-campus;
- the need to accredit prior learning;
- the need to build generic or personal transferable skills into courses;
- the move towards strategic alliances beyond the university; and
- changing career paths for academic staff.

WIDESPREAD AVAILABILITY OF COMPUTER-BASED ACCESS TO INFORMATION

Although it has long been obvious to librarians, information specialists and computer experts that we are on the brink of an entirely new dispensation with respect to widespread public access to information, it is only in the past couple of years that discussions about the information superhighway have infiltrated most mainstream academic discourses. Today, however, it is virtually impossible to escape mention of the Internet and the World Wide Web, and how these ubiquitous technologies promise, or threaten, to revolutionize academic work.

Much of the hype concerning the information superhighway is, of course, overstated, and may be likened to earlier 'fads' such as personalized instruction, teaching machines, or the much-vaunted computer-aided instruction movement of previous decades. While there is clearly an element of infatuation about the information superhighway, there is little doubt that the pervasiveness, accessibility and appeal of computer technology sets this particular 'wave' apart from its predecessors.

Although the full promise of the Internet may lie some years in the future, there are still enough contemporary intimations of its potential that higher education cannot afford to ignore its possibilities for the delivery of instruction. Neither can we afford to ignore the even greater significance of the extraordinary power which it offers individuals actually to bypass formal educational providers in favour of finding things for themselves.

With respect to the first of these issues, the proliferation of both CD-ROM technology and of interactive media such as the World Wide Web offers the opportunity not only to revolutionize much teaching, through allowing for the asynchronous delivery of material at the learners' convenience, but it also expands the potential reach of educational institutions. In future, universities will be able to compete more or less on an equal footing with other local and international providers, thus rapidly internationalizing the education and training marketplace. It also means that education, perhaps more than ever before, might have to compete with entertainment for people's in-home attention, with implications for the quality and accessibility of ideas being provided.

Turning to the issue of learners choosing to bypass formal educational institutions, the same technology brings much information within the reach of just about anybody who has a computer and Internet access. As has been repeatedly pointed out, data is not knowledge, and the Internet cannot replace what has been dubbed 'the extended voice' of scholarly argument; nevertheless, universities and other formal education institutions are going to have to radically rethink their role as gatekeepers and as conduits to knowledge. This is particularly vital in areas of professional learning, where there is a growing sense of impatience among certain people with what is seen to be the unduly slow and abstract processes of higher education compared with the rapidly changing realities of the workplace.

INCREASING DIVERSITY IN THE STUDENT BODY

As the higher education system has expanded, inevitably a more diverse range of students has been drawn into university-level study. Many students for whom degree study would not previously have been an option are now to be found in university lecture theatres and laboratories. These include those whose families have no experience of higher learning, who may therefore lack the 'cultural capital' traditionally associated with going to university, and those with relatively low tertiary entrance scores, who are correspondingly less well prepared for advanced study. In addition, universities have deliberately sought to recruit overseas students (largely as a way of supplementing their income, but also out of conviction that this will lead to a richer on-campus student mix), along with those representing minority groups (such as people from certain religious or ethnic groups, or women in subject areas traditionally dominated by men) and those having various disabilities.

While all this has undoubtedly led to a more diverse, colourful and representative student body, it has multiplied exponentially the challenges for teachers, especially when – as previously mentioned – undergraduate class sizes have grown significantly. Staff, most of whom lack formal preparation as teachers and who are also under pressure to perform in a more diverse range of professional activities, are now expected to deal with students who:

- may not speak or write English as well as necessary to pursue their studies;
- lack basic foundational knowledge;
- lack necessary support or appropriate study habits at home;
- are in a minority and feel alienated from other students;
- lack the financial resources to buy books, personal computers or other aids to learning, or to attend necessary field trips;
- are mature-aged and have not been in formal education for many years; or
- are in a variety of other ways, different from some imagined 'norm' (which in many cases is an abstract ideal, or a stereotype, anyway).

THE DEMAND FOR OFF-CAMPUS LEARNING

For many students, full-time on-campus study is neither a desirable nor a practical option. For instance, there is increasing pressure for many people who are already in the workforce to upgrade or to retrain entirely; yet financial costs and family responsibilities may preclude them from regular on-campus attendance. For others in geographically isolated locations, the preference to stay with family and friends may be strong, with the result that university level studies might be possible only through learning at a distance. Some overseas students may choose to return to their own cultures and to their work, family or civic responsibilities as soon as direct face-to-face teaching is no longer needed. For others again, the desire to learn at work or at home might derive from the need to have access to specialized equipment or resources, or from a particular lifestyle or learning style choice. For all these, and many other reasons, a greater number of students are electing to complete some, or even all, of their studies independently through open learning or on the Internet; through courses that may be available to them in their workplace; or maybe via local further education or community colleges under some franchise arrangement.

Many universities, recognizing these trends, have embraced flexible programming, whereby students have much greater autonomy in terms of what, when, where and how they learn. Many have entered into agreements with large employers to provide university-level courses through the employers' (or, in the case of professionals, through the professions') existing networks and infrastructure. Others have made use of new technologies, video-tapes, audio and video-conferencing, computer discussion groups and the World Wide Web. In Britain, for instance, and in some cases in Australia, arrangements have also been made with local colleges or other universities to offer part or all of their programs on a contract basis, with suitable quality control mechanisms to ensure adequate standards of instruction and of assessment.

THE NEED TO ACCREDIT PRIOR LEARNING

The combined effect of the previous two considerations (increased diversity among students and a preference for learning while earning) has been to force universities to consider how their courses might be more flexible and responsive. One aspect of this is that many students, especially those designated as 'mature-aged', come to their studies with a wealth of knowledge and skill, which might have been obtained in a range of ways: on the job; through travel, family, or private reading; by independent study; or through attendance at other short courses. In all these cases, it is quite reasonable for students to expect that they will not have to learn again something that they have already mastered.

Whereas previously universities might have been able to dictate to students the requirements for successful completion of their courses, including presenting formal assessment in areas already familiar to the student, today, learners are more mobile, more demanding and more informed. It is reasonable that an experienced person seeking, say, a degree in engineering, would shop around to see which institution would give the greatest credit, or advanced standing, for his or her prior learning. Similarly, once enrolled in a degree program, the more sophisticated learner will commonly seek exemption from those aspects of the course that he or she has already mastered. Accordingly, it is vital for universities to have in place:

- very clear statements of learning outcomes at each of three levels – courses, units, and even topics or modules within units;
- excellent and accessible academic advisers to assist students to meet the structural and other requirements of courses; and
- robust, objective and consistent mechanisms for granting credit for prior learning, including prior experiential or unaccredited learning.

THE NEED TO BUILD GENERIC OR PERSONAL TRANSFERABLE SKILLS INTO COURSES

One of the global shifts in higher education has been the move towards more professional training. Generalist degrees (such as BA, BSc, etc) are giving way to – or at least being coupled with – professionally oriented qualifications in Business, Law, Engineering, Information Science, Architecture, Town Planning, etc. At the same time, employers and professional associations are becoming much clearer and more demanding about the learning outcomes they expect from such courses, if graduates are to be permitted to practise. Not infrequently, these two principles are in tension with one another: on the one hand, employers and professional bodies are insisting on a greater concentration of 'technical' content in the degrees, yet on the other, they are giving preference to graduates who are broadly educated, flexible, able to communicate well, good team members, etc.

As mentioned above, one response to this pressure has been to undertake double degrees, but this can be costly in both economic and personal terms. Another approach has been to build such generic or personal transferable skills into courses, either as direct instructional content or, not infrequently, into the way in which the courses are taught, structured and assessed. Such skills and attributes as communication, teamwork, self-organization, lifelong learning, information literacy and leadership, however, cannot simply be written into a 'wish list' of programme objectives. It is essential that they are embedded in the structure of courses and, above all, that they are assessed alongside other aspects of the course content. In the UK, for instance, much has been done, not only in terms of how to teach and to assess such accomplishments, but also how to validate or authenticate this parallel set of learning outcomes in student exit statements.

THE MOVE TOWARDS STRATEGIC ALLIANCES BEYOND THE UNIVERSITY

A recent book by Gibbons, Limoges, Novotny and others entitled *The New Production of Knowledge* (1994), raises the important point that:

'A multi-billion dollar knowledge industry has developed outside established educational institutions, responding in more direct, and usually more effective ways, to the needs of industry and the labour market. This is leading to the erosion of the monopoly the universities have enjoyed in providing training and granting educational credentials with good currency in the private sector.' (p.76)

Australia has not escaped this trend; indeed in a 1990 paper entitled 'The Demise of the University in a Nation of Universities', Mahoney argues:

'much of the pursuit, analysis and manipulation of the knowledge seen to be highly relevant by society now occurs outside universities. This includes the most taxing and sophisticated investigations in fields as diverse as scientific, agricultural, health, technological, engineering, business and economic research.' (p.457)

In addition to this shift in research, the previously mentioned widespread direct availability of masses of information on the World Wide Web is already changing, and has the potential to change further, the dissemination of knowledge and even to alter how people choose to learn. One particular feature of this global shift in both knowledge production and distribution is the move towards greater transdisciplinarity. Both individuals *and* organizations increasingly need information to solve complex real-world problems, in the context of rapid and pervasive social, cultural, legal, political, economic and technological change. Historic disciplinary boundaries and borders are being blurred, and even dissolved, in both teaching and research. Accordingly, universities need to seek strategic alliances with other parts of the knowledge industry in both teaching and research, and, within themselves, interdisciplinary (and flexible) courses and programmes will increasingly supplant rigidly compartmentalized programmes of study.

CHANGING CAREER PATHS FOR ACADEMIC STAFF

The so-called 'casualization' of the academic workforce – in which universities are increasingly relying on part-time, casual and sessional staff, and
whereby the sanctity of tenure has been seriously questioned – has been a
source of increasing concern, especially to academic unions and to staff
developers. Although there are clearly grounds for serious disquiet,
especially when this casualization involves the exploitation of relatively
powerless staff numbers and the erosion of social criticism as part of the
academic role, its effects may not be altogether negative, especially in cases
where staff members mix their teaching and research duties with continuing
experience in other (appropriate) workplaces. Indeed, the relevance,
immediacy and flexibility of courses is often enhanced when academic staff
members can draw on recent experience in the workplaces for which
students are being prepared. At the opposite end of the continuum,
especially at the upper reaches of the university, many members of staff
may lack recent relevant experience outside academia, with the result that
they are out of touch with the 'real world' of business, industry or the
professions.

In an interview with *Campus Review* (1–7 February, 1996) the recently
appointed Vice-Chancellor of the University of Queensland, Professor John
Hay, commented that a large percentage of the community's intellectual
strength is currently not located in universities. He went on to say:

> 'I am absolutely certain that unless and until Australian universities have that
> relationship with the business and professional downtown communities,
> where they move easily in and out of universities by adjunct appointments,
> then we will never catch up with what the leading universities in North
> America are doing.' (p.3)

The practice of academics moving in and out of universities is by no means
an exclusively North American phenomenon; British and European
universities, too, are bringing outside expertise in and sending their staff
out to mutually enrich the institution and the community which is served
by the university. However, for such practices to be more than just occasional
curiosities, universities will need to loosen their personnel policies, and
issues such as staff development and superannuation have to be more
flexible and responsive to facilitate the easier transition of staff (including
adjunct faculty) in both directions.

SOME IMPLICATIONS FOR ACADEMIC DEVELOPMENT

As mentioned at the outset, these are only a few of the most pressing changes that are impacting on higher education institutions at present. No doubt there are others, and no doubt at least some institutions have already developed excellent ways of anticipating and dealing with such trends and issues. Nevertheless, academic developers might care to give consideration to some or all of the following matters.

- The need to establish, if they do not already exist, integrated language and learning skills units to support part-time and full-time, English-speaking and non English-speaking, undergraduate and postgraduate students.
- Staff development in dealing with diversity, especially in the student body, but also in the academic workplace itself.
- More flexible and permissive course structures, and agency agreements that allow the offering of awards through other providers including further education and community colleges, or in the workplace.
- Greater exploitation of flexible delivery mechanisms, including the Internet and World Wide Web, and support for staff wishing to develop and offer learning opportunities in open learning mode.
- The need for all course units to have clear and unambiguous learning outcomes against which claims for exemption or advanced standing based on the recognition of unaccredited prior learning might be assessed.
- The need for extensive training in how to identify, develop, assess and verify generic or personal transferable skills, as well as mechanisms for validating or authenticating their attainment, principally at the undergraduate level.
- Much greater attention to cross-disciplinary courses and programmes of study, and more permissive course regulations to encourage students to take units outside their major faculty or disciplinary domain.
- Increased use of adjunct and part-time staff, along with appropriate staff development and career development for such people.
- The possibility of offering 'externships' to enable members of regular academic staff to maintain their links with industry or the relevant professions.

Clearly this list is far from exhaustive, but it might offer initial ideas to those who are attempting to develop a flexible, responsive and proactive approach to staff and educational development.

CONCLUSION

In a recent paper in the *International Journal of Academic Development* (Candy, 1996), I ventured a seven-part model of academic development, of which one element was that it must be 'anticipatory'. By this I meant that it must go well beyond simply reacting to changes that we have already experienced, and indeed even beyond adjusting quickly to changes that we are currently experiencing. Instead, anticipatory academic development involves constantly scanning the horizon and seeking to prepare people for likely futures before they arrive.

Such working at the margins between the present and the future has its risks, and sometimes we will get it wrong. This, however, is no excuse for not trying. In 1989, I wrote a paper entitled 'Didactomancy: Anticipating the Academic of the Future'. Looking back at that paper now, the striking thing is neither how accurate the prediction was, nor how hopeless it turned out to be; rather, that many of the predictions and observations I made then are still current and contemporary. In other words, despite the dramatic changes that have undoubtedly swept the field of higher education, many of the central features of academic work have surprisingly not changed all that much... at least not yet. I concluded that paper with this observation:

> 'It seems, then, that it is simplistic and misleading to speak of *the* academic of the future as if there were only one... Instead, it seems more appropriate to consider the *academics* of the future (plural); to acknowledge the many different views held by those who are or will become university academics; to recognise the necessary interdependence of different parts of the academic role (both individually and corporately); to uphold the traditional diversity and loose linkages that characterise universities worldwide; and to affirm that although universities are changing their outward shape, they continue to have a special place and role in modern society.' (Candy, 1989, p.32)

It seems to me that the challenge for academic developers is how to maintain a balance between the best of traditional scholarly values and practices on the one hand, and the seemingly inexorable and irresistible demands for change and innovation on the other. In many respects, this is precisely the same dilemma confronted by academics in the disciplines as well: acknowledging the rapidly changing dynamics of the 'real world' while at the same time, being prepared to challenge the headlong and often non-reflective pursuit of 'relevance'.

As competition intensifies, not only between institutions but indeed between universities and other providers, it is apparent that there may be areas in which universities can respond more flexibly, more innovatively, and more proactively than at present. Issues such as comprehensive support for students in developing all types of academic and technological literacy, exploiting the enormous educative potential of the World Wide Web, enhanced flexibility in course structures and enrolment patterns, greater attention to the development and assessment of generic skills and attributes, the recognition of unaccredited prior learning, and entering into strategic alliances with other providers of education and training, are all worth careful consideration.

Attention to these and other emerging issues could help to ensure that academic developers provide flexible, responsive and forward-looking programmes and, in turn, that their institutions will continue to be attractive to potential students, staff, benefactors, government, employers and to research and teaching partners.

REFERENCES

Candy, P C (1996) 'Promoting Lifelong Learning: Academic Developers and the University as a Learning Organization', *International Journal for Academic Development,* **1**, 1, 7–18.

Candy, P C (1989) 'Didactomancy: Anticipating the Academic of the Future', in *Research and Development in Higher Education,* Vol. 12, G Mullins (ed.), Higher Education Research and Development Society of Australasia (HERDSA), Campbelltown, NSW.

Clark, B R (1989) The Academic Life: Small Worlds, Different Worlds, *The Educational Researcher,* **18**, 5, 4–8.

Coyne, A (1996) 'Privatize or Perish: The Case for Blowing up our Ivory Towers', *Globe and Mail (Toronto),* 4 May.

Gibbons, M, Limoges, C, Novotny, H, *et al.* (1994) *The New Production of Knowledge: The Dynamics of Science and Research in Contemporary Societies,* Sage, London.

Mahoney, D (1990) 'The Demise of the University in a Nation of Universities: Effects of Current Changes in Higher Education in Australia', *Higher Education,* **19**, 455–72.

Chapter 18

Facing up to Radical Changes in Universities and Colleges

Sally Brown

This book is about radical change in the academic context. For the individual working in universities and colleges, this can mean trying to reconcile a wide range of conflicting and overlapping pressures which include the following.

- **Accepting transformations of job descriptions** at regular intervals, with the old certainties of what it means to be a member of the academy swept away.

- **Learning to live with new reporting relationships**, as reorganizations and restructuring exercises move from hierarchic structures to matrices (and back again).

- **Losing substantial elements of autonomy**, especially about how and when work is undertaken and how the different elements of work are balanced.

- **Coping with a changing (often worsening) work environment** when physical space in many institutions is at a premium, buildings are frequently under-maintained and demands for ever-improved equipment and technology increase.

- **Learning to use new technology to support teaching and learning** at times when it seems that the ink is barely dry on the instruction manual (which is often incomprehensible in any case).

- **Trying to work out who the customer is** in a service-orientated context and trying to satisfy all the (sometimes conflicting) demands of stakeholders including students, parents, employers, the government, quality agencies and others.

- **Taking responsibility for line management of others**, sometimes without the necessary authority to take meaningful decisions, to offer rewards or to use sanctions.

- **Managing a devolved (and often shrinking) budget**, frequently with very little training for the task and dire penalties for errors.
- **Accepting a high level of ambiguity and uncertainty** with concomitant stress levels.
- **Working ever faster in a competitive environment**, trying to be more efficient and effective in work practices when all others in the marketplace are doing likewise.
- **Pursuing the relentless quest for continuous improvement**, since quality enhancement is the goal we are all urged to strive for and since professionals want to do their best for those for whom they work and are responsible.

Facing up to all of this is a pretty tall order. Elsewhere I have written about the conflicting pressures on academics to ratchet up their research output (in the UK to satisfy the Research Assessment Exercise) while at the same time to demonstrate the excellence of their teaching, and this can frequently leave us feeling dissatisfied with our own levels of achievement in either domain (Brown and Smith, 1996). Unsurprisingly, stress levels are often high in universities and colleges. Despite Stephen Cox and Ruth Heames' suggestion in Chapter 15 that a certain amount of stress is a useful stimulus to good performance, we all can recognize that there can be too much of a good thing.

Working patterns are changing with research and preparation time being eaten into by additional duties. The headline from a *Guardian* article on piloting the use of third semester teaching at Luton University trumpeted 'Goodbye to the Long Vac' (Kingston, 1996), but in reality for most university staff, vacations just mean it is slightly easier to park and that the type of work being undertaken is rather different.

The rate at which change is taking place makes it difficult for us to keep on top of the issues let alone to develop appropriate strategies. Finegold *et al.* (1992), reporting on a seminar in 1991, postulated a situation in the year 2000 where the proportion of 18-year-olds in higher education would reach one in three: in fact this proportion was achieved within a year of publication of the book. They envisaged a buoyant growing sector providing a non-elitist mass system of higher education, whereas at the time of writing, the sector is buffeted by winds of change much stronger than we would have believed possible even five years ago.

Student numbers are now no longer growing at the 'Russian vine' rate they were, the unit of resource is still being driven relentlessly downward, morale in many universities is plummeting, as the over fifties feel the hot breath of early retirement at their necks and the rest of us watch our backs for the next wave of redundancies, reorganizations and restructuring exercises.

Added to this, there are requirements to respond to a much more diverse student body, who can be both more demanding and yet simultaneously less motivated than previous cohorts, as Pauline Kneale has suggested earlier in this book. Even the most saintly academics, administrators, librarians or technicians can feel their patience sorely tried by stroppy students when they feel under pressure themselves. We see them for shorter periods of time since modularization, we know them less well than we did even five years ago since we tend to see them in ever larger groups, and we find it even more difficult to recognize their needs, because they seem to be even more varied.

Academics who have spent their life developing an area of expertise and who regard their key tasks as creating knowledge and keeping on top (or ahead) of their field, do not take kindly to being told in a postmodern way that content is dead (or at least strictly time-limited), that their lectures are likely to be superseded by electronic means of course delivery and that their roles as university teachers have changed from being lecturers to facilitators of collaborative enquiry as described by Lorraine Stefani and David Nichol in Chapter 13. This Copernican shift (Brown and Smith, 1996) has taken the lecturer from the centre of the universe and has placed there instead the students who may not at first sight be all that inspiring. Such a change of status, as Pete Sayers and Bob Matthew describe in Chapter 14, while potentially liberating, can be disconcerting.

Librarians and computing services personnel often find that their roles are converging towards a role of information support provider and that the perceived safety of a known working environment is being eroded, as new demands are made upon them and continuous professional updating becomes a survival strategy. Technicians too are seeing their jobs change, for example, from audio-visual support staff to multimedia production officers, and higher levels of skill and flexibility are being asked of them than ever before. It is not uncommon for universities to offer extended opening hours for libraries and IT centres, and it is the support staff rather than the academics who primarily service these functions.

Administrators similarly are being asked to cope with different working patterns, with transforming roles (for example in the demand for them to use IT and the expectation that they should be working towards NVQ qualifications) and they find themselves with steadily increasing workloads. Many universities are keen to see the administrative burden taken off the academics so they can be more productive in teaching and research, but there is often little recognition of the extra load this puts on the administration. At the same time, administrators are often (erroneously) viewed as superfluous to core business so are first in the firing line when job cuts are suggested.

Mortimer (1996) quoting Nias and Biott (1992) has compared the effects of such disruptions to a working environment to the grieving process, with those in the midst of upheaval withdrawing, expressing anger and becoming demotivated. Describing a substantial institutional merger, she suggests that radical change can be felt as depowerment, can reduce commitment and loyalty and can drastically affect productivity.

Many UK universities (and this is reflected too in Australia and New Zealand as well as elsewhere internationally) have an atmosphere within them in which forward planning appears futile because the situation changes hour by hour, where the uncertainty principle rules and where the whole basis on which we have built our academic and professional careers seems to be under attack. How then can we face up to not only these radical changes but to the practical, emotional and professional fall-out that ensues?

I suggest that three principles must support our actions, as we explore ways to turn what feel like monstrous threats into opportunities to maintain personally and professionally satisfying careers and a productive and enjoyable learning environment for our students.

1. *Any radical change that is proposed solely as a cost-cutting exercise is likely to be doomed to disaster*

If we introduce resource-based learning, or peer assessment, or matrix structures for management or flattened hierarchies only because they will enable us to save money, they are likely to damage the quality of the institution and the programmes we offer.

Resource-based learning offers wonderful opportunities to transform radically the way in which we structure and deliver learning programmes (Brown and Smith, 1996) but requires substantial up-front investment of time and money if it is to be effective, and will take regular maintenance if it is to remain viable. Gibbs *et al.* (1994) undertook research into the ways in which resource-based learning could be used in a range of disciplines and concluded:

> 'In the current harsh economic climate, much resource-based learning [RBL] is introduced in order to save money (or at least, lecturer's time) rather than to increase flexibility or to improve educational effectiveness. However, RBL is not automatically cheaper: it often has hidden costs and requires additional, unforeseen extras if it is to work effectively: and it requires resources that may not be readily available, such as space for students to study in. Before embarking on large-scale investment in RBL, it is prudent to examine a range of resource implications.'

Peer assessment can be an invaluable element in the repertoire of assessment methods available to lecturers to help students become more self-aware about their learning achievements (Brown and Knight, 1995) but it does not provide a quick fix for the academic who wishes to get rid of the chore of marking.

Matrix structures that make departmental organization more effective and flatter organizational hierarchies that shorten command chains and remove superfluous levels of management can be effective at improving intra-organizational communication and increase motivation and output when effectively implemented, but clumsy organizational hatchet work erodes productivity and saps morale.

Universities have demonstrated over recent years that it has been possible to make efficiency cuts without destroying the organism from which the savings are shaved, but there is no substitute for strategic planning and forward investment. While the Japanese government is doubling state support for research and development, other countries are slicing funding down to the irreducible medium. Cassandras among us have to restrain ourselves from mentioning the experiment on equine nutrition where the researchers had just managed to get the horse to survive on one wisp of straw per day before it died.

2. Universities are not factories with production lines, nor are they financial corporations with the sole aim of making money

We need to decide whether we are interested in richer universities or richer learning environments as our prime focus. An anecdotal story from a management conference for a large industrial company has the managing director telling his employees 'we're not here to make steel, we're here to make money'. Universities' core business, however, is not making money, but creating and disseminating knowledge, even though we have to be canny with our finances if we are to survive. It can be easy in the current adverse financial climate to lose sight of what it is we are really trying to do, leading to decision-making based on cash equations rather than research or learning gain.

We can borrow from the rhetoric of industrial quality models, auditing our systems and processes, examining our customer-care features, writing mission statements, practising kaizen and adding value, but we cannot adopt them wholesale without the loss of much we hold dear. We cannot hope for a nil defect model in student achievement, for example, if we wish to maintain our access policies enabling all who can potentially benefit from what we have to offer to enter our august portals to study. Employees can adopt new work habits for a radically changing world (Pritchett, 1994) but collective as well as individual responsibility is important.

3. Universities must retain a human face

Universities are essentially people-centred and they cannot function if the humanity of the organization is lost. This is not to argue for cosy arrangements which apocryphally existed in previous eras, with tutors and students sipping sherry in segregated commonrooms and the one-to-one tutorial as the prime medium of teaching. However, we need to ensure that the radical changes we make in universities and colleges do not make it impossible for students to congregate, associate, argue, deliberate, share experiences, interact in groups and gossip with each other and with staff, either in person or virtually if necessary. If we pare down the curriculum delivery function to putting our notes on the World Wide Web or into learning packages, if we replace spoken and written communication with solely electronic means then valuable elements of the education process are lost.

If we convert association areas like commonrooms into open access IT centres, if we shut our office doors outside few, highly regulated hours and have voice mail to replace a friendly person on the end of the phone, if the library becomes a function rather than a place and the photocopier no longer retains its 'village pump' identity where people can stop and gossip because it's all done by electronic fibre straight to the students' rooms, then we might as well all be working for multinational corporations or as teleworkers in our own homes.

Radical change in colleges and universities is to be welcomed when it enhances the quality of students' learning and when it enriches the experience of those who work within the system. It is important that our working practices are effective and efficient, but we need to ensure that a genuine principled rationale is in evidence for every innovation, modification and transmutation of the higher education systems of which we are justifiably proud.

REFERENCES

Brown, S and Knight, P (1995) *Assessing Learners in Higher Education*, Kogan Page, London.

Brown, S and Smith, B (eds) (1996) *Resource-Based Learning*, Kogan Page, London.

Finegold, D, Keep, E, Miliband, D Robertson, D, Sisson, K and Ziman, J (1992) *Higher Education: Expansion and Reform*, Institute of Public Policy Research, London.

Gibbs, G *et al.* (1994) 'Course Design for Resource-Based Learning Project Materials', Oxford Centre for Staff Development, Oxford.

Kingston, P (1996) 'Goodbye to the Long Vac', *The Guardian*, Higher Education section, 9 July, p.3.

Mortimer, J (1996) 'Easing the Process of the Merger Situation', Unpublished research, University of Northumbria at Newcastle.

Nias, J and Biott, C (1992) *Working Together for Change*, Open University Press, Milton Keynes.

Pritchett, P (1994) *The Employee Handbook of New Work Habits for a Radically Changing World*, Pritchett and Associates Inc, Washington DC.

Smith, B and Brown, S (1995) 'Research, Teaching and Learning: Issues and Challenges', in *Research, Teaching and Learning in Higher Education*, B Smith and S Brown (eds), Kogan Page, London.